The **4 CORE** Factors
for School Success

Todd Whitaker
Jeffrey Zoul

EYE ON EDUCATION
6 DEPOT WAY WEST, SUITE 106
LARCHMONT, NY 10538
(914) 833-0551
(914) 833-0761 fax
www.eyeoneducation.com

Library of Congress Cataloging-in-Publication Data

Whitaker, Todd, 1959-
    The 4 CORE factors for school success / by Todd Whitaker, Jeffrey Zoul.
        p. cm.
    Includes bibliographical references.
    ISBN 978-1-59667-090-7 (alk. paper)
1. School management and organization. 2. Educational leadership. 3.
School improvement programs. I. Zoul, Jeffrey. II. Title. III. Title: Four
CORE factors for school success.
    LB2805.W475 2008
    371.2—dc22

                                                          2008021474

Composition by
UB Communications, Parsippany, NJ

Also available from Eye On Education

What Great Principals Do *Differently*:
15 Things That Matter Most
Todd Whitaker

Study Guide: What Great Principals Do *Differently*
Beth Whitaker, Todd Whitaker, and Jeffrey Zoul

What Great Teachers Do *Differently*:
14 Things That Matter Most
Todd Whitaker

Study Guide: What Great Teachers Do *Differently*
Beth Whitaker and Todd Whitaker

Seven Simple Secrets:
What the BEST Teachers Know and Do!
Annette Breaux and Todd Whitaker

Dealing with Difficult Teachers, Second Edition
Todd Whitaker

Improving Your School One Week At a Time:
Building the Foundation for Professional Teaching
and Learning
Jeffrey Zoul

Cornerstones of Strong Schools:
Practices for Purposeful Leadership
Jeffrey Zoul and Laura Link

What Great Principals Do *Differently* DVD
Featuring Todd Whitaker

What Great Teachers Do *Differently* DVD
Featuring Todd Whitaker

*The authors would like to dedicate this book
to their respective mothers,
Avis Whitaker and Jerri Zoul,
both of whom provided a strong foundation based
on deeply-held core values.*

*To my mom, thank you for your patience,
kindness, and caring.*

– Todd

*To my mom, thank you for teaching me
the importance of gratitude, forgiveness,
and empathy.*

– Jeff

About the Authors

Dr. Todd Whitaker is Professor of Educational Leadership at Indiana State University in Terre Haute, Indiana. Prior to coming to Indiana, he was a middle school and high school principal in Missouri. A former math and business teacher at the Junior High level, Dr. Whitaker also served as middle school coordinator in Jefferson City, Missouri. Dr. Whitaker is the author of numerous books, including the highly-acclaimed *What Great Teachers Do Differently*, *Dealing With Difficult Parents*, and *What Great Principals Do Differently*. Dr. Whitaker is a highly sought-after speaker who has made over 1,000 presentations at the state, national, and international levels. He is married to Beth, a former teacher and principal, who is an associate professor in the Elementary Education Department at Indiana State University. They are the parents of Katherine, Madeline, and Harrison.

Dr. Jeff Zoul is a principal with North Shore School District 112 in Highland Park, Illinois. Prior to becoming principal at Edgewood Middle School, Dr. Zoul served as a teacher, coach, assistant principal, and principal at the elementary, middle, and high school levels in the State of Georgia for 26 years. In addition, Dr. Zoul served as an adjunct professor of graduate studies at North Georgia College and State University. He is the author of *Improving Your School One Week at a Time: Building the Foundation for Professional Teaching and Learning* and co-author of *Cornerstones of Strong Schools: Practices for Purposeful Leadership* and *Study Guide: What Great Principals Do Differently: 15 Things that Matter Most*. Dr. Zoul has presented at national conferences on a wide variety of educational issues. He earned his doctoral degree from the University of Alabama and holds additional degrees from The University of Massachusetts at Amherst, Troy State University, and The University of Southern Mississippi. Jeff is married to Jill, a middle school teacher, and they are the parents of Jordyn. Please contact Jeff at author@eyeoneducation.com.

If you would like information about inviting the authors to speak to your group, please contact Todd at t-whitaker@indstate.edu or at his website www.toddwhitaker.com or (812) 237-2904. Contact Jeff at jeffzoul@comcast.net or (847) 432-3858, ext. 209.

Table of Contents

Chapter One
Clarifying Your C.O.R.E.

Many years ago, Thomas Jefferson wisely proclaimed: "In matters of style, swim with the current; in matters of principle, stand like a rock." This advice still rings true today, particularly for those in the field of education, where—at times—it seems as if matters of style threaten to interfere with sound educational principles. Together, we have amassed over 50 years of experience at all levels of the educational spectrum. In these years, we have seen many "matters of style" ushered into schools with a great deal of fanfare only to give way in a year or two to another new fad. Although we have accepted many of these changes in style over the years, adapting our practice however slightly to do so, we have held fast to our core beliefs and principles throughout. Early in our careers, each of us realized that educational programs would come and go. Some of these programs seemed fairly effective while others seemed less successful. Secretly, we always suspected that the variable in terms of program success was not so much the program itself as the person charged with implementing the program. This observation led to Todd's oft-quoted comment that it's "people, not programs" that make a difference (Whitaker, 2004, p. 9). Although these programs tended to change frequently, the people—primarily teachers and principals—required to implement them typically remained on the job, adjusting on an annual—and seemingly cyclical—basis to the latest program initiative. Although ushering in a steady stream of such changes proved frustrating, we were both able to "swim with the current" on those occasions. Part of our success in doing so is that we were steadfast in adhering to our core principles, relentlessly reminding ourselves what was really important in spite of whatever changes might have been occurring around us.

In earlier books, Todd (Whitaker, 2003 & 2004) wrote about the importance of every teacher and principal clarifying their own core values. This is essential for the success of any educator, particularly in today's public school setting, where so much of what we do seems to be in a constant state of flux. In order to not only survive, but thrive, as an educator truly focused on what is most important, we must rely on our core principles to see us through the shifting currents of style. We realize that every teacher and school administrator reading this book is a unique individual, working in a unique school setting, with a wide variety of diverse challenges and rewards. Each of us is faced with a litany of choices on a daily basis. Our educational principles are what guide us when faced with an onslaught of what could otherwise prove an overwhelming number of challenges and tough decisions. Whether you are a teacher or an administrator working at the elementary, middle, or high school level, in an urban setting, or in a small rural school, you are faced with monumental tasks each and every day, and we encourage you again to reflect on and clarify what lies at the core of your educational philosophy. What is it that comprises the very essence of you as an educator? We maintain that although great educators vary in numerous ways, there are a few core principles that they all have in common and that contribute to overall school success.

In addition to creating a list of core principles on which we stand to guide us through times of change and conflict, we must also share these openly and regularly with others. Teachers must share these with their students, with their parents, with their teaching colleagues, and with their administrators. Administrators must also share their core principles with everyone in the school community, particularly every teacher (a term we use to include all adults at the school who come in contact with—and, therefore, teach—students; cafeteria workers, custodians, and secretaries teach our students wonderful lessons every day) working within the school. Although we have written and presented on a wide variety of topics in recent years, we learned—while collaborating on a previous project—that we share four particular core principles in common. In working with thousands of teachers and school leaders across the country, we came to realize that the very best among them also emphasized these principles in their classrooms and throughout their schools. We began discussing the importance each held for us, how each of the four had played a major role in any successful ventures in which we had participated, and how one or more of these principles had been overlooked in less successful initiatives. These discussions became the genesis for the ideas contained in this book. As we kept returning to the theme of clarifying those core principles we held in common, we also realized that they coincided nicely with the very word "core" itself, and we introduced the acronym C.O.R.E. to stand for our four most important and enduring principles of success for both teachers and school leaders: Communication, Observation, Relationships, and Expectations (Zoul & Link, 2007). We consider each of these four factors relating to all levels of education "matters of principle," and we continue to stand, as Jefferson advised, like rocks in ensuring that we purposefully act in ways that emphasize our beliefs related to these simple—yet powerful—principles.

Defining and Discerning the Core

American Heritage (2000) defines the word *core* as "the central, innermost, or most essential part of anything." In education, if we were to survey hundreds of practitioners, we would likely receive various responses as to what constitutes the core of our profession. Certainly, "learning" is a primary focus of our business, as are test scores, student behavior, student attendance, and dropout rates. However, these core components of education are all *outcomes* we aim to impact over the course of a school year. In order to produce desirable outcomes, we must concentrate on our ABCs: the actions, behaviors, and commitments we exhibit on a daily basis that may have a positive impact on these critical school outcomes. Nearly all educators we know entered our noble profession because they wanted to make a difference in the lives of young people. The actions we take as teachers and administrators do make a difference, particularly in the educational outcomes listed above. While the primary "business" of schools may well be student learning, we firmly believe that our behaviors related to communication, observation, relationships, and expectations (the 4 C.O.R.E.) dramatically impact how much learning will occur—on the part of both students and educators. By identifying specific strategies in each of these four areas that teachers and administrators can easily employ at their schools throughout the school year, we believe that significant educational outcomes—most importantly, student learning—will improve.

Each of the core principles discussed throughout this book is as much a human relations skill as it is a teaching and learning skill. In all walks of life, successful people are strong communicators who are careful observers of the world around them. They build positive relationships in their personal and professional lives and maintain high expectations for themselves as well as for those with whom they interact. Despite the multitude of changes facing those of us in the education profession, at least one constant remains: ours is a people-focused venture. To succeed as professional educators, therefore, we must master the "people" skills of communicating effectively, observing and monitoring carefully, building positive personal and professional relationships, and establishing clear expectations for ourselves, our students, and each other.

Enduring Principles of School Success

For years, we have maintained that it is our people, not our programs, that make the difference in our schools. In our experience, this has remained one constant in the ever-changing milieu which is public education. In recent years, we have worked with teachers and administrators at schools that have enjoyed great success and attributed their success to a wide range of initiatives that were undertaken at the school level. However, we are also familiar with schools that have undertaken these identical initiatives and failed miserably. The variable, of course, is not the program being implemented, but the people enacting the implementation. Successful educators adhere to core principles that guide their daily actions resulting in higher levels of school performance.

Programs in education—even those with great initial promise-often prove fleeting. On the other hand, the principles we value as educators endure. In our experiences at hundreds of schools across the nation, the 4 C.O.R.E. principles of Communication, Observation, Relationships, and Expectations have stood out as the most enduring principles of all as exhibited by high-achieving educators working in high-achieving schools. People focused on these school success factors can make nearly any program successful. Meanwhile, no program will succeed if the people implementing it are not focused at their very core on these enduring principles so vital to the success of any venture. Our aim in this book is to focus on the behaviors our very best educators exhibit that align with these beliefs: in what ways do educators consciously committed to the 4 C.O.R.E. factors act differently than others in order to produce the most dramatic results in terms of overall learning?

From Principles to Values

The enduring principles of school success—communication, observation, relationships, and expectations—are neither esoteric, theoretical, grounded in scholarly research, nor solely applicable to the realm of education. In addition, these principles are not inherently actionable; that is, we must examine each of these and decide how we will act to ensure that we purposefully address each of these in our daily professional routines. We must move from the *belief* that these principles are important to *behaviors* that produce results. In other words, we must move from *principles* in which we believe to *values* upon which we will act. DuFour and Eaker (1998) suggest that values are essential to overall school success and school improvement. They challenge those within the organization to "... identify the specific attitudes, behaviors, and commitments they must demonstrate in order to advance..." (p. 88). For each of the 4 C.O.R.E. principles related to enduring school success, we created five values statements that compel those within the school to commit to behaving in ways that make these principles a reality. What follows, then, is a list of 20 actions related to the school success factors of communication, observation, relationships, and expectations to which educators within the school can commit to adhering. These actions are applicable to both teachers and school administrators, who must work together to ensure that these values are enforced.

Communication

♦ *We Will* systematically and regularly communicate our Mission, Vision, Values, and Goals to all school stakeholders.

♦ *We Will* communicate the results we are achieving as a school throughout the school year to all school stakeholders.

♦ *We Will* communicate with each other about the work we are doing in our individual classrooms and throughout the school.

♦ *We Will* communicate with our students, informing them of their own progress, including areas of strength and areas in which they need further improvement.

♦ *We Will* communicate regularly and systematically with all parents informing them of their child's progress.

Observation

♦ *We Will* observe our students carefully, monitoring individual learners, noting and responding to their unique learning capabilities and learning needs.

♦ *We Will* observe each other in the classroom in order to gain new insights into best practices and provide constructive feedback.

♦ *We Will* observe events occurring in our community, which may also impact our school.

♦ *We Will* monitor our progress toward school improvement goals on a daily basis and adjust our practices based on what we observe.

♦ *We Will* monitor the time we spend each day on specific behaviors relating to teaching and learning, ensuring that our behaviors are aligned with research-based best practices.

Relationships

♦ *We Will* cultivate collegial, collaborative conversations by scheduling purposeful planning sessions.

♦ *We Will* demonstrate an awareness of each other's personal, as well as professional, lives, acknowledging significant events and accomplishments and remaining informed about personal issues affecting professional performance.

♦ *We Will* rely on face-to-face interactions between teachers, parents, administrators, students, and community leaders whenever possible.

♦ *We Will* celebrate individual student and teacher success, as well as school-wide success regularly and systematically.

♦ *We Will* confront those within the school community who are not acting in accordance with our mission, vision, values, and goals with honesty, fairness, and a desire to effect positive change and growth.

Expectations

♦ *We Will* establish and enforce clear expectations for student behavior and student academic performance.

♦ *We Will* expect our students to succeed, and we will intervene strategically and immediately when they are not.

♦ *We Will* establish and enforce clear expectations for all educators within the school, holding ourselves accountable for adhering to our stated values.

♦ *We Will* expect our parents and others within the school community to work as partners with educators in ensuring that our students perform to standards.

♦ *We Will* expect each other to uphold all school policies, yet realize that individual teachers may create additional expectations for themselves and their students that they will create and enforce.

The statements above are a first step in moving from one-word principles of success to action steps that stand as core school values—commitments to behaving purposefully in order to improve school and student performance. Still, these 20 commitments are broad statements of action without specifying precisely how they will be carried out. In the remaining chapters of this book, we will offer specific strategies that we have used or observed in hundreds of schools and that address these statements, providing educators within the school a clear roadmap for acting in a manner consistent with these principles and values.

The 4 C.O.R.E. School Success Factors

There are literally hundreds, perhaps thousands, of factors that lead to the success—or lack of success—in our schools. Differentiation, assessment for learning, professional learning communities, mentoring and induction, standards-based grading and reporting, standards-based unit design, inclusion of special education students, and sheltered instruction for English Language Learners are just a few of the recent educational buzzwords that we happen to agree are valuable ways to improve our schools. Yet, in a bigger-picture sense, the 4 C.O.R.E. principles of communication, observation, relationships, and expectations are even more crucial to school success because they are necessary human relations skills that must be purposefully and consistently acted upon if any of the other school programs listed above are to succeed. No school improvement initiative can succeed in a school unless the educators within that school are accomplished in these four critical areas.

In the following chapters of this book, we will provide specific steps for teachers and school leaders interested in improving their skills in these four vital areas of education and promoting behaviors that fulfill these responsibilities. Every strategy we share in this book has been successfully implemented in elementary, middle, and high schools across the country. Perhaps the best thing about these ideas is that they are simple. We all have the ability to do them. They can be implemented in any classroom at any school immediately. The difference between mediocre educators and great educators is that the great ones will not only acknowledge them; they will act upon them.

Chapter Two

Communication: Strategies for Success

The importance of communication in any organization cannot be overstated. Stephen Covey goes so far as to state, "Communication is the most important skill in life" (1989, p. 237). In perusing any job posting or job description, one can almost assume that "strong oral and written communication skills" will be included as a skill necessary for the position advertised. Effective communication skills are especially vital to school success, where teachers, administrators, students, parents, and community stakeholders must all be aware of what occurs within the school setting. Teachers and school administrators must excel in all facets of communication to ensure a safe and orderly learning environment, a sound instructional program, and optimal levels of learning for students. Educators skilled in the area of communication recognize these multiple facets of this trait and purposefully plan for fulfilling all components of this core responsibility outlined below in a systematic, consistent manner.

Facets of Communication		
The imparting or interchange of thoughts, opinions, or information by speech, writing, behavior, or signs.		
Educators effective in the core skill of communication:		
♦ *Advise*	♦ *Disclose*	♦ *Read*
♦ *Articulate*	♦ *Disseminate*	♦ *Receive*
♦ *Assert*	♦ *Exchange*	♦ *Reveal*
♦ *Attend*	♦ *Express*	♦ *Speak*
♦ *Care*	♦ *Inquire*	♦ *Teach*
♦ *Connect*	♦ *Listen*	♦ *Tell*
♦ *Converse*	♦ *Make Known*	♦ *Translate*
♦ *Correspond*	♦ *Notify*	♦ *Transmit*
♦ *Declare*	♦ *Publish*	♦ *Write*

Teachers cannot expect results from the students they teach if they do not effectively communicate precisely what it is they want students to know and be able to do at the outset. Similarly, school administrators must communicate to teachers what must be done and the ways in which the work must be carried out.

Both teachers and school administrators spend almost every minute of the day engaged in the act of communication, specifically the actions listed above. Whether we are in front of the classroom teaching students, conducting a faculty meeting, or simply walking around the cafeteria, we are communicating a great deal about our beliefs, expectations, and attitudes. The way we speak, read, listen, walk, sit, stand, and dress sends both explicit and subtle messages to those on the receiving end of our varied communications. It is vital that all educators realize the extent to which communication impacts their likelihood of success in the schoolhouse and discover ways to improve their skills in this area.

Sommers (2007) identifies two primary responsibilities related to communication for principals. We maintain that these apply to teachers as well: (1) lead conversations on instruction and learning and (2) keep hope alive. As educators, it is imperative that—regardless of our specific role—we consistently engage others, including our students, in discussions about learning. The responsibility to keep hope alive may be a less obvious, but even more important, component to communication. Teachers and administrators are—in a very real sense—in the business of "hope." Although it may sound trite, we often talk about the dreams we have for our schools and our students while cultivating within students their own dreams for future success as well as actions for fulfilling these hopes and dreams. The way we communicate with our students and with each other plays a major role in keeping these hopes and dreams alive.

Effective Communication Defined

The National PTA (1997) offers six standards for family involvement programs, listing "Communication" as its first standard and suggesting that effective communication between the home and school must be regular, two-way, and meaningful. Although stated quite simply, we feel that this three-pronged approach to communication—regular, two-way, and meaningful—is not only the key to successful home-school communication, but also the key to communication in every other school relationship, including—most importantly—principal-teacher, teacher-teacher, teacher-student, principal-student, and student-student. All three components of this definition are essential to fulfilling this core responsibility related to school success, and we will offer specific ways for educators to communicate regularly, meaningfully, and in an open, two-way manner.

McEwan (2003) suggests that effective communicators must have the capacity to empathize, interact, and connect with each other and with all school stakeholders. They must be able to teach and present information and motivate people with whom they interact. Reeves (2006) also suggests that all within the organization must possess effective communication skills. While he acknowledges the increasing importance of high-tech forms of communication, he also argues for holding on to the non-technological side of communication, such as handwritten notes. He characterizes effective communicators in today's organizations as "... simultaneously high tech and high touch, maximizing their reach through technology, as they optimize their effectiveness with the encouragement, appreciation, and nurturing that only a personal handshake, hug, note, or the spoken word can provide" (pp. 59–60). We echo Reeves's words and find that in effective schools with positive school cultures, the teachers and administrators working within the school are regularly engaged in such "high touch" forms of communication to an even greater degree than those forms of communication that could be considered "high tech."

Marzano, Waters, and McNulty (2005) found the skill of communication to be one of 21 responsibilities school leaders—including administrators and teacher-leaders—can execute effectively that ultimately lead to improved student academic achievement. They suggest that this responsibility encompasses all the ways the school leader establishes strong avenues of communication between and among both students and teachers, as well as the extent to which the school cultivates and maintains vehicles for communicating to and from parent and community stakeholders. Finally, in her findings published in 2003 examining the relationship between principal behavior and student achievement, Kathleen Cotton (2003) identified 25 categories of principal actions that positively affect several school outcomes. Not surprisingly, she describes one of these categories as *communication and interactions*. In addition, of the remaining 24 categories, nearly every one—such as *emotional and interpersonal support*—also involves some aspect of this overarching responsibility of communication.

The research showing that great schools are filled with great communicators is abundant and overwhelmingly clear. In addition to this research, together we have amassed over 50 years of experience working with schools from the elementary level to higher education and presenting at conferences throughout the United States. From the research we have examined and the experiences we have collected, we find the skill of communication to be one of four core responsibilities of both teachers and school administrators. Because of our strong belief that good communicators produce better school outcomes, we have intentionally emphasized specific, strategic communication practices throughout our careers. What follows are just a few ways we have found in which teachers and school leaders can employ specific communication strategies to improve student and school performance. The strategies we have outlined below require very little of the practitioner, other than a commitment to move from knowing they are important to actually following through and implementing them at their schools. Each suggestion below is rather simple to understand and implement and can be used at the elementary, middle, or high school level. In addition, we offer ideas for teachers and administrators, as well as ideas that pertain to both groups of educators.

Starting and Ending the Week

Two ideas that we have used at the middle and high school level and that are also ideal for elementary school educators are ways to begin and end the week with a powerful and consistent form of communication. One of these focuses more on the operational aspects of the specific school week, while the other is a teaching and learning communication, focusing on a selected topic relating to education. We call the former our "Thank God,

It's Monday" memo and the latter is known as our "Friday Focus." The "Thank God, It's Monday" (TGIM) memo is an email sent out to all staff first thing Monday morning (or even over the weekend, for teachers who check their email outside of school) that can include a variety of information but that always includes a detailed schedule of every event occurring at the school that week. In addition to the week's schedule of events, the TGIM can be a vehicle for highlighting staff birthdays, teacher accomplishments, the school's mission and vision, student successes, statistics related to education, and even a faculty trivia contest.

As a middle school and high school principal, Todd would place a hard copy of the TGIM in each teacher's mailbox at the start of each week. More recently, Jeff has been emailing a similar version to teachers at a middle school for several years. Teachers at these schools quickly became accustomed to reviewing the TGIM both for critical information about upcoming events as well as simply to learn more about the students and teachers with whom they worked. Although we aim to include important information relating to school that week so that no one is surprised by any interruptions to instructional time or fails to attend an important after-school event, we also include a great deal of information just for fun, keeping in mind that our foremost goal is for teachers to read this important memo each week. While the format changes slightly over the course of a school year and from year to year, below is a sample TGIM sent to staff as they were returning from the winter holidays to begin a new semester:

Teachers: Thank God, It's Monday!!!

Our Mission: Our unrelenting quest is to do Whatever It Takes to teach, inspire, and motivate all learners!!!!
. . . . Thanks for working together so well and so hard last semester; our efforts have paid off and will continue to pay dividends in terms of student learning as we move through this new semester. . . . As we begin the new semester, now is a good time to clearly review our

expectations for student learning and student behavior. Then, let's all commit to strengthening our relationships with students so that they will *want* to meet our expectations in these areas! . . . Thanks to Joanie & Jody and all who helped as we selected our 2007 Geography Bee winner. Thanks also to Wendy and all who helped in coordinating our spelling bee program! . . . Thanks to everyone who nominated a colleague for Teacher of the Year. We received nominations from 20 teachers in total with just a few repeats. Clearly, we are staffed with a multitude of TOTYs. . . . Good luck to our 8th grade students on this week's writing assessment. All our Language Arts teachers have done a fabulous job preparing our kids to be proficient writers. Our success in this area is well documented, and I anticipate another stellar performance this year . . . **play** . . . **make their day** . . . **be there** . . . **choose your attitude.** . . . Have an awesome week; teach with passion:

Random Fact to Contemplate:

Take your height and divide by eight. That is how tall your head is.

Graduation Fact from Randi:

In October, 1998, there were 3.9 million 16 through 24 year olds who were not enrolled in a high school program and had not completed high school; this represents approximately 12 percent of the entire age group.

This Week's Stuff:

Monday:	************	Final Round 6th Grade Spelling Bee
	7:45 & 4:30	Drama Tryouts
	8:15	Equestrian Club Meeting
	4:15	Equestrian Team Meeting
	4:15	4H Horse Quiz Bowl

Tuesday:	7:30–8:30	PLC Small Group Meetings
	4:30	Drama Tryouts
	8:00	4-H Club Meeting
	4:20	CDT Club
	5:00	BBALL: 7th Grade @ SFMS
	7:00	Parent/Community Forum (FCHS)
Wednesday:	***********	Drama Callbacks
	7:45	Tech Club
	8:00	Academic Team Meeting
Thursday:	7:30–8:50	Leadership Team Meeting (Conference Room)
	1:30–2:00	Writing Assessment Training (Sloop's Room)
	8:00	Advanced Chorus
	10:30	Spelling Bee (Media Center)
	5:00	BBALL: 8th Grade @ SFMS
Friday:	***********	School Elimination for Oratorical Contest
	***********	Relay for Life Hat Day!!!!!!
	8:00	Academic Team Meeting
	8:15	FCA Meeting
	8:00	Writing Assessment Training (Media Center)
Saturday:	10:00	BBALL: all 4 teams @ Lumpkin County

Happy Birthday!!!

Upcoming Birthdays:
Ginger, January 8th!!!!
Patti, January 9th!!!
Tiffany, January 11th!!!

The Essential 55: Rules for Discovering the Successful Student in Every Child by Ron Clark (2003):

Rule 49: Be positive and enjoy life. Some things just aren't worth getting upset over. Keep everything in perspective and focus on the good in your life. *(Ahhhh . . . more good advice for us all, particularly as we begin a new school semester and calendar year. The other day when Dr. M. had us line up in order of our level of optimism toward the coming year, I laughed and marveled to see many of you—notably Coach H— jockeying for position as the most optimistic teacher among many world class optimists. Although in general, I consider myself an optimistic person, I confess that at times I focus too much on the negative and things beyond my control. I resolve to do better in this area and remember Ron Clark's advice. Here at our school, we work about as hard as humanly possible to resolve all conflicts and problems that inevitably arise. The truth is that we are successful the vast majority of the time. There are definitely many things we can control, influence, and change. Yet other things remain which are beyond our control, problems or difficult situations with no easy answer. All we can do in these instances is deal with such issues as best we can, take the pressure off ourselves, and move forward. I am proud of our relentless "can do" spirit at our school; at the same time, I encourage you to focus on the positive in all areas of your life even when that means realizing not everything which occurs is something we can control).*

Faculty Trivia Question (Free Prize for First Correct Answer):

Which staff member jumped from a plane 10,000 feet and dove down 130 feet under the Gulf Stream to a shipwreck, though no treasure was found???????????

   (a) Tracie   (b) Leslie   (c) Rachael   (d) Wanda

As important as it is to begin each week by communicating with all staff about the events occurring at the school, we find it even more important to communicate our ideas, reflections, expertise, and opinions about issues related to teaching and learning in a consistent and systematic manner. At our schools, we have used a weekly *Friday Focus* memo to accomplish this goal. Todd (Whitaker, Whitaker, & Lumpa, 2000) first shared the idea of a weekly staff memo called the *Friday Focus*. Since that time, many principals and teachers at all grade levels around the world have shared their practices in this important area of communication, culminating in Jeff's (2006) book, which compiled 37 *Friday Focus* memos written by him and many teachers and leaders at his school on a wide variety of educational topics.

The Friday Focus is simply a short (usually between 750 and 1,000 words) writing on a selected topic that is crafted and sent out (typically via email) to all staff every Friday morning. Many of these should be written by the principal and assistant principals, but we have also sent out versions written by teachers, central office leaders, outside experts, and even our school secretaries. We consider every adult who works in our building a teacher, since they are working around young people and, therefore, teaching in a direct or indirect way something about life and learning. We find the Friday Focus to be a perfect way to close the week in terms of professional communication at any school. By this point of the week, most of our "Thank God, It's Monday" items have been crossed off our to-do list, and we are excited about the upcoming weekend. We have found that a very high percentage of our teachers take the time each Friday to start the day by reading the insights being shared that week. Often, the Friday Focus sets in motion a discussion among teachers regarding the issue being examined. At times, the author of the week's Friday Focus will invite others to visit their classroom to observe firsthand what it is they are sharing. At other times, Friday Focus authors will include useful attachments to the memo or let others know that they will be leaving related information or resources in the teacher workroom. Depending on the school and situation, sending out the Friday Focus and allowing others to read it at their leisure can be the extent of this communication vehicle. On the other hand, schools have used these memos as something to study further in faculty meetings, team meetings, and professional learning community meetings. The extent to which schools use the Friday Focus can vary widely, but at a minimum, it is a relatively simple and consistent way for those within the school to exchange ideas and initiate discussion about our profession.

At our schools, we have adopted a format for the Friday Focus that we follow each week. First, we start off with a quote that relates to the topic of the memo. Next, we simply write about the topic, including thoughts based on our experiences as well as any research on the topic we feel is worth sharing. Finally, we often close with examples of teachers within the school who might already be experts in this particular area. Below is a recent example of a Friday Focus on the topic of "Building Background Knowledge," which follows this format:

B

Friday Focus!

Friday, August 24, 2007

"Although the extent to which students learn new information is dependent on many factors, research supports one compelling fact: what students *already know* about the content is one of the strongest indicators of how well they will learn new information relevant to the content"

(Marzano, R. J., 2004).

Last Friday, I wrote about Active Learning as an instructional focus for the letter "A." In Barbara Blackburn's book, *Classroom Instruction from A–Z: How to Promote Student Learning* (2007), the author chooses "Background Knowledge" as the chapter topic for "Chapter B." I was excited that this was her topic for the letter "B" partly because of my passion for Marzano's work related to Building Background Knowledge and, especially, Building Academic Vocabulary (BAV). For those who are new to our school or may have forgotten this method for teaching academic vocabulary, I am attaching the BAV handout we created last year.

Blackburn calls background knowledge—or the knowledge our students already have—the foundation for any new learning they will acquire. We need to know what they already know (or think they know) before we can build on that foundation of learning, taking them from where they are, to where they need to be. She offers a few strategies for understanding and building this background knowledge. The most common way is a KWL or a variation of KWL she calls LINK:

L *List* everything you know
I *Inquire* about what you want to know
N *Now* we are going to take notes
K What do you *Know* now?

In addition to these familiar methods of building upon background knowledge, Blackburn shares two other simple ideas worth mentioning: (1) *Sticky Notes:* as students enter class hand them a sticky note. A question on the board asks them to write what they know about a new topic to be studied. Students respond on sticky notes and place on board. The teacher reads every sticky note, verbally acknowledging each, perhaps categorizing them on the board, before moving forward with additional teaching and learning about the topic at hand; (2) *Sharing What We Know:* have students work in small groups to write facts about a particular topic on a sheet of paper. As the paper comes around, each student writes one thing they already know about the topic and passes it along to their neighbor. The paper continues around the small group circle, a second or third time, if appropriate. When the group has exhausted all thoughts, have groups switch papers, reading another group's list to see whether they can add to it. They will more than likely see something new, too, that they had not thought of.

Background knowledge is the foundation for all future learning. Our students come to us with wildly varying levels of background knowledge based on the number and frequency of academically-oriented experiences they have had and their ability to process and store information. Outside of school, we are not able to impact the former, but we have a huge impact on the latter. We must discern where our students are before we can advance them to a new level of understanding. Students will retain information better if we connect it to those prior experiences they might have. There are many strategies we can employ to learn where our kids are and how we can best connect where they are to where they need to be.

If you have a chance next week, stop by to conduct an OMS Peer Observation Report on Mike, Beth, or Lee Anne to see how they are incorporating LINK strategies into their lessons. Understanding what our students already know and connecting this background knowledge to new information we want to present is another way we commit to *Teaching with Passion!*

Happy Weekend————Jeff

The Friday Focus above manages to communicate a few key tenets relating to the importance of background knowledge, referencing two educational works on the topic and including specific pockets of excellence already in place at this particular school. In addition, Jeff shares some of his personal experiences and philosophies in terms of background knowledge. Finally, he encourages teachers to observe each other (using an "OMS Report," which is explained in Chapter Three) in the near future to focus on various ways teachers at the school are using strategies related to background knowledge. We have found the Friday Focus—if used consistently and systematically—to be a relatively simple and highly effective way to communicate with all teachers at the school what is occurring in our classrooms and what we are learning about best practices, both within the school and from our outside research. Since the Friday Focus comes from *within* (i.e., the teachers, administrators, and other school leaders are the ones sharing their insights), we find it to be more credible. Teachers tend to trust and respect the ideas of those working within the building who are having success more so, perhaps, than what they hear from an outside "expert."

Great principals and great schools have in place communication vehicles for making certain that each teacher in the school knows what is occurring each week. In addition, they have systems in place for exchanging ideas about teaching and learning best practices with each other. Beginning the week with a Thank God, It's Monday memo and closing each week with a Friday Focus memo for teachers to read and reflect upon are two specific ways that schools can accomplish the goal of communicating important information with **SUCCESS** because they are both:

Simple
Unique
Credible
Consistent
Empowering
Systematic
Shared

These weekly communications contain all the above characteristics that help to cultivate a community in which all stakeholders work collegially to heighten awareness of important events and information. We encourage you to try these two tested methods in your own schools.

The Good, The Bad, and The Ugly

Some teachers and administrators with whom we have worked are adept at communicating good news, yet are uncomfortable or unwilling to communicate not-so-good news. On the other hand, it seems that some educators are quick to communicate bad news but rarely take time to share good news about students, teachers, administrators, and events within the school that are making a positive difference. In schools that consistently and positively impact student achievement, teachers and administrators within the building make a concerted effort to communicate all aspects of their performance among each other and with their students, parents, and other stakeholders. The purpose of communicating the good, the bad, and the ugly— whether we are talking about an individual student's behavior or school-wide performance on an important standardized test—is not to paint an overly rosy scenario nor to be excessively critical of underperformance. Instead, it is simply to get at the truth in terms of current status so that we can move forward and achieve greater results.

One example of an issue facing educators that requires an honest assessment and willingness to communicate current status as well as subsequent progress is that of student discipline. This is an inevitable concern of many educators; it seems we are forever trying to "improve" our students' behavior. One of the most effective ways we can do so is by first clearly communicating our expectations in this important area of school success. Then, we must communicate with our students, their parents, and each other on a regular basis precisely what it is we are observing related to student behavior. Too often, our attempts at communication in such matters are limited to complaining with our colleagues about the ongoing problems we are having with a particular student or even an entire class. Not only is this a waste of time and energy, it is also ineffective in resolving the problem. A more effective way for resolving student misbehavior is by communicating—with other teachers, administrators, parents, and students themselves. Other teachers who know the student may have insights into successful strategies for working with a particular child. Administrators, too, may have information that can help. At times, we overlook the most obvious stakeholder: the student. Sometimes, finding the time to conference privately with students about their behavior can be very revealing and helpful in effecting change. Finally, communicating with parents about their child's behavior can be the most productive of all avenues for achieving positive results. Although at times it may not seem like it, we have found that nearly 100% of parents want their children to behave at school. Some parents are better equipped than others in helping to make this hope a reality, but every parent of every child would likely state that they expect their child to behave appropriately. Every teacher and administrator at every school we know of wants every parent to support them in enforcing behavioral expectations. At first glance, then, it would appear that both parties are on the same page and that no conflicts could possibly arise, since both parents and educators want kids to behave. Sadly, this is not always how things work, and the problem often lies in the area of how we communicate. It is our job as educators to communicate with parents in such a way that makes them *want* to support our efforts to improve their child's behavior. We start by communicating honestly, regularly, and positively.

Communicating with parents about their child's behavior can, of course, take many forms and a multifaceted approach is often best. We have worked with many educators who successfully use emails, phone calls, written notes, conferences, and post cards sent home to communicate news regarding student behavior. All can be effective tools for communicating with parents, yet—not surprisingly—the communication *method* we employ is not nearly as important as the *manner* and *regularity* in which we communicate it. We should communicate regularly with our parents, not just when we experience a problem with their child's behavior. Parents are much more likely to support our efforts when we have established a regular system of communicating with them. More importantly, we should communicate in a positive manner with our parents regarding their child's behavior—whether the news falls into the good, the bad, or the ugly category. Communicating good news would seem an easy enough proposition, yet, too often, we fail to do this. Many years ago, Todd employed a positive discipline referral program at a school where he served as principal, whereby he called parents of students who had been cited by someone at the school for behaving in a positive manner. At times, the student being "referred" was a student who consistently behaved well. On the other hand, he often met with students who regularly misbehaved but had been "caught doing good" by some teacher at the school. Todd always made it a point to immediately call the parents of any student who was referred to his office for good behavior.

Jeff has also used a systematic positive discipline referral program in schools, complete with an official "referral" form which looks very similar to the regular—and more common, in most schools—discipline referral form. This form even has space allocated for "Actions Taken by the Principal" as a result of the referral. Typically, Jeff will include: (1) Referral sent home (2) Phoned parent (3) Free ice cream within this space. In a middle school with nearly 1,000 students, Jeff typically received over 350 positive discipline referrals each year. This simple communication strategy dramatically changed the culture of the school. The Positive Discipline program is one of the few ideas we know of that takes almost no effort on the part of teachers yet positively impacts not only teachers, but also students, parents, and the principal. Each time we recognize a student for a positive discipline referral, the student is happy, the parent is thrilled, the administrator is happy to be dealing with good behavior, and the parent often calls the teacher to thank them for "writing up" their child!

Although it may be more enjoyable to communicate good news about student behavior, we must also communicate with parents when their children are not behaving. As educators, we must not allow ourselves to merely complain about student behavior or moan about lack of administrative support in dealing with behavior problems. Instead, we must communicate clearly and consistently to students and parents our expectations for student behavior. Of course, we must also establish positive relationships with our kids and parents so that they will want to meet our expectations. In our own experience, we have found ourselves calling parents about their child's unacceptable behavior after we have previously called to let them know their child had received a positive discipline referral. It is amazing how supportive parents are in such instances: they know that we have taken the time to communicate the good, not just the bad and the ugly. As a result, we have found that parents are much more willing to support us in working to correct misbehavior. When communicating with parents regarding a child's misbehavior, we feel that schools should establish a certain amount of consistency. First, we feel that whenever possible, such communications should be made either in person or over the phone in a conversation. Leaving voicemails or sending emails describing a child's misbehavior is rarely, if ever, advisable. In addition, administrators and teachers should work together at the outset of each school year to determine agreed upon standards for contacting parents about student misbehavior. Regardless of how long the administration and faculty have worked together at a school, this must be addressed annually. Each school will need to agree on their own guidelines, of course, but every educator in the school should commit to a general outline of communication behaviors they will agree to such as:

(1) *Call Early*   We should open the lines of communication between the school and parents as soon as possible in the school year, especially when we detect potential behavior issues which may inhibit learning.

(2) *Call Often*   We should follow up on these early phone calls, either letting parents know that the concerns have been allayed or that they are continuing and further interventions are necessary.

(3) *Be Honest*   We should always be direct and honest about any negative behaviors we are observing, yet we should also deliver this news in a positive manner, treating parents and students with dignity and respect and emphasizing that we are here to help the child succeed in improving his/her behavior.

(4) *Find the Good*   We should always find good news to share with parents when we are also pointing out concerns we have regarding their child's behavior.

(5) *Listen*   We should always actively listen to the parents of kids we teach. Regardless of any family situation, the parent knows their child better than those at the school

and is aware of their strengths, needs, interests, and desires. By genuinely listening to parents, we may learn new ways to connect their child to the school. In addition, by simply listening to our parents, they know that we care about them and will be more willing to support our efforts.

Although we have thus far focused on communicating with parents regarding both "good" and "bad" news dealing with only one area of student performance (behavior), the possibilities for fulfilling this responsibility are endless and all educators must follow through on communicating regularly with parents about all aspects of their child's school performance.

We are strong advocates for consistently communicating with parents regarding the good, the bad, and the ugly, yet we also realize the need for educators within the school to meet regularly to address the same in terms of school performance. Instead of focusing on the somewhat easier task of assessing *student* actions and performance, we must address the actions that *we* are taking which impact—either positively or negatively—student outcomes. At our schools, we have found it beneficial to meet as a whole faculty every six weeks in an open-forum format to discuss what we call, again, the good, the bad, and the ugly. We even begin these meetings with a short slide show of photos recently taken at our school which illustrate each. Typically, of course, we will include a photo or two of an administrator or superstar teacher or coach in some less-than-flattering, but humorous, pose to represent "the ugly." On a serious note, we may include a slide that shows our attendance as the lowest in the system to represent "the bad" or a slide of a teacher working alongside a student to represent "the good." After this ice breaker, we simply elicit open-ended responses from all staff regarding what is working, what is not, and what needs to be looked at further or in a different way. Almost all educators talk about desiring honest and open communication between all teachers and administrators working within a school. Such communication can only occur in an organization marked by trust.

Convening regular meetings to share opinions on how we are doing certainly affords us the opportunity to communicate with each other. However, the way in which we receive and act on this news will determine the efficacy of the communication and the level of trust. After sharing both good and bad news about our schools, we must process this information in some way. One suggestion is to reach consensus on one positive idea that was shared which all staff might try to implement or learn more about. At the same time, we should try to agree on one item which merits our immediate attention as an area needing improvement. It may be something as mundane as hallway supervision or dress code issues or something more directly related to student achievement, but it is important to walk away with a sense that all educators had a chance to share their views while reaching consensus on at least two important issues relating to school performance.

One a Day; One a Week

Although nearly everyone would agree that communicating regularly with our students, our parents, and each other is vital to school success, it is amazing how often we fail to follow through in a systematic manner on this core responsibility. Pfeffer and Sutton (2000) have written persuasively on the idea that a knowing-doing gap exists in the corporate arena. That is, companies *know* what works and what they should do, but often fail to *do* the very things they know will work. We suspect that this knowing-doing gap is equally evident in schools. The area of communication is but one glaring example in which we fail to consistently do that which we know we should. When we ask educators why they do not always do the things they know they should, we almost always receive the same response. No one ever states that they simply enjoy being a slacker or relish the idea of being known as an insubordinate resistor. Instead, almost always we hear that there is simply not enough time in the day to do everything. Ironically, there always seems to be enough time in the day for us to complain, gossip, send humorous emails, and schedule personal appointments, yet the nasty issue of "time" keeps rearing its ugly head as an obstacle to fulfilling much more important responsibilities. To be fair, nearly all educators we know do work extremely long hours and are swamped with a daily deluge of scheduled and unscheduled tasks to accomplish. As a result, we must find a manageable and consistent system for regularly communicating with and among students, parents, and each other. Taking a cue from the vitamin folks, we suggest a "One a Day" approach or a "One a Week" approach, depending on the type of communication we are making.

Postcards Home. One way for teachers and principals to communicate with students and parents which takes very little time and which has worked with great success at many schools is to mail postcards home sharing good news about a student. The cost of such postcards is minuscule—or may even be free through business partners or school photography companies—and the impact can be powerful. Although we tend to think of email as a much more efficient and easy way to communicate, a written note mailed home is much more personal and much more meaningful—both to our kids and their parents. As far as the time required, each educator in the school can commit to the "one-a-week" postcard sent home as a minimum. To do so requires perhaps five minutes of time. Teachers and administrators will quickly agree that the return on this small investment of time is well worth it. Administrators should arrange for the school to provide postage and, if possible, pre-printed mailing labels with student addresses. Many teachers with whom we have worked find that writing one or more postcards to a student and/or parent at the very close of each week not only establishes a routine but also works as a positive, uplifting way to end the work week. By simply committing to writing one postcard each week, every teacher in the school will have sent personalized good news home to 35 or more students during the school year.

Phone Calls Home. Teachers and administrators should also make it a point of emphasis to call parents each week. As a starting point, we again recommend the "one-a-week" standard as a minimum, with each educator in the building committing to placing one positive phone call home to a parent along with one phone call a week home to a parent of a student who is experiencing academic or behavioral difficulties. The positive phone calls home are fairly easy and actually fun to do, as parents tend to be happily surprised by this unexpected practice. So often, they will respond with something along the lines of, "I've never had a school call me with good news before!" Placing such calls come with absolutely no downside. Both the educator making the call home and the parent receiving the call feel better as a result.

Placing a different type of phone call is not always as pleasant but may be even more important. We simply *must* maintain constant and personal contact with parents of students who are struggling. We must speak in a manner which is positive and respectful, but we must also be specific and honest about the concerns we have. In addition, we must provide strategies for addressing those problems we are describing. If every educator in the school makes just one of each type of phone call weekly, the school as a whole will be widely recognized as one that makes an impact in the area of communication. For example, in a school with 50 certified staff, 100 parents will hear—in a personalized format—from the school about their child's successes or struggles each week throughout the year.

Note Cards to Teachers. A simple practice that each administrator at any school can implement on a "one-a-day" schedule is to communicate positive comments to teachers by writing one note card every school day of the year—which, for most schools, is 180 days. If a school has even two administrators in place, this means that 360 cards will be written throughout a school year thanking and praising adults within the school for their service. Even with a total staff of 200—including custodians, cafeteria workers, and office personnel—a strong probability exists that each staff member will receive one or more cards from an administrator throughout the year.

Although this may seem like an ambitious undertaking, carried out consistently, it requires no more than ten minutes each day. Administrators can purchase inexpensive blank note cards at dollar stores at the beginning of the year. Although methods for writing these daily notes can vary from school to school, the focus should remain the same: to communicate, in writing, any type of positive news we know regarding one of our teachers. At times, these words may be a follow-up to an effective lesson observed during an informal classroom visit. Administrators might also write to thank a teacher for sponsoring an extracurricular activity or congratulate a coach for an important victory. We may write to teachers thanking them for mentoring a first-year teacher or going the extra mile for a student in need. The content can vary; but we try to be brief, yet praise a very specific behavior or accomplishment in a genuine manner. Some administrators write one card each morning upon arriving at school. Others write them at home or during a visit to a teacher's classroom. Regardless of when they are written, afterwards administrators can simply place these in teachers' mailboxes or leave them on teachers' desks. At schools where administrators have practiced this, teachers appreciate the fact that someone has taken time to personally recognize them in this simple way.

As we said at the outset, "lack of time" is the reason most would give for not doing a more thorough job of fulfilling their responsibility to communicate regularly as educators. Though time is always a nagging issue, we feel that it is more a matter of priority than time that interferes with our intention. By following a "one-a-day" or "one-a-week" approach to communicating with parents, students, and each other, we can make a positive impact in an important aspect of our school's culture. More importantly, we ultimately optimize the performance of our students by providing consistent feedback in these ways.

Teacher Newsletters

As important as it is for administrators and teachers to communicate in writing consistently with each other, it is equally important that teachers communicate weekly in writing with the parents of the students they teach. Although most teachers will and should communicate with parents in a variety of ways throughout the school year, we have found it imperative that all teachers send out a weekly newsletter informing parents of the week's activities, learning goals, homework assignments, and test dates. Although some successful teachers write and distribute an individual weekly teacher newsletter, we have found that it is often more effective and efficient for teachers to send these weekly parent newsletters home as a team. At the elementary level, this might be done by grade level while at the middle-school level, newsletters might be sent out by interdisciplinary teams. At the high school, we suggest sending these out by department. At each of the three levels, consistency in format is a key to success. Each teacher member of the grade level, team, or department should include the same core information about the teaching and learning that will occur in their classroom during that particular week. In addition, each newsletter from the entire school should include information regarding school events (such as those outlined in the Thank God It's Monday in the previous section). Oftentimes, teacher newsletters will also include information from the Media Center, PTA, club sponsors, coaches, and even a memo from a school administrator. Finally, the teacher newsletter is an effective way to thank parents for supporting school rules and policies that arise as areas of concern each year.

In terms of distributing teacher newsletters, clearly each school is unique, with varying parent needs and means of accessing information. Often, the teacher newsletter can be sent home weekly via email. However, not all parents have email access, and it is important to provide hard copies for parents who prefer receiving the newsletter in this way. While we cannot guarantee that every parent will read every newsletter we send out, we *can* guarantee that we will make the effort of communicating in this way. There are ways we can enhance the chances that parents read our teacher newsletters. The more useful and user friendly our parent newsletters, the more likely it is parents will read them. In addition, if we involve our students in the newsletters in creative ways, parents may be more likely to keep up with them. Ensuring that the teacher newsletter is distributed at the same time each week, with a consistent framework of information included helps parents anticipate the newsletter and what to look for within. Finally, as with most things we do, we have found that if we in some way incorporate just a bit of fun into teacher newsletters, parents are more likely to look forward to reading it. Do not be afraid to include inspiring quotes, amusing anecdotes, a word of the week, or a solicitation for parent input. Communicating with parents regularly and systematically is a must for any teacher and any school that aims to succeed at impacting student performance. The teacher newsletter is a means of establishing a year-long communication device between school and home.

School Newsletters

In addition to ensuring that individual teachers or teams of teachers send weekly newsletters home to students and parents, schools should send home a monthly or semimonthly newsletter home to all families. The scope, print quality, and method of delivery for such newsletters will vary greatly depending on many variables including school size and budget, but it is imperative that all schools communicate to families about the "bigger picture" events occurring within the entire school community as well as what is occurring in individual classrooms. As principals, we both sent out monthly newsletters to our communities, informing all stakeholders about important events. In addition to mailing—or emailing—such newsletters to all homes with students attending our schools, we also sent these communications to business partners, community leaders, school board members, central office personnel, and principals at neighboring schools.

At one middle school, the school mascot is the "Bullpup," and each month the school sends out an edition of the *Bullpup Bulletin*. Each edition of this newsletter includes information about business partners, school clubs, athletic events, yearbook, transition activities, the media center, fundraising efforts, counseling programs, the Parent Teacher Organization, performing arts, and the nature and characteristics of adolescents. In addition, every newsletter begins with a letter from the principal, updating students and parents on a few points of emphasis each month. Although the newsletter in total tends to be fairly lengthy, a sample of a "Letter from the Principal" is included below from a December edition of the *Bullpup Bulletin*:

Letter from the Principal . . .

Dear Parents and Students:

With just the tiniest amount of disbelief, I note that the holiday season is now in full swing. This is often a time of joy, family, gifts, reflection, and even a bit of panic. Although a wildly busy time for us all, it is extremely important that we remain focused on teaching and learning while school is in session during these final few weeks of our first semester. Like most students, I rejoice in the holiday frenzy throughout the month of December, yet I also view these final weeks before our vacation as a prime opportunity for learning. This year, we actually have a few extra days of school compared to past years, with Friday, December 21, 2007, standing as our final day of school for this first semester. We have had an awesome one thus far; let's all focus on **working hard** for a few more weeks followed by a concentration on **having fun** during the holiday break!

I have bragged often and loudly about our phenomenal teachers. I have been equally effusive in my praise of our students, yet I wish to highlight their efforts once again. Our students are remarkably mature, polite, and respectful young people. Each morning, hundreds of them continue to greet me at the front door by extending their hands, looking me in the eye, and using my name as they wish me a hearty, "Good morning!" In addition, I have met with over 200 students so far this semester in my office to commend them for being recognized by a teacher with a Positive Discipline Referral. It is an honor to be associated with a school widely known to be filled with such respectful and caring students.

Students, thank you in advance for my holiday gift: making my days rewarding and enjoyable. Parents, thank you for raising such outstanding children.

Parents, each year I ask our staff to recommend holiday gift ideas that parents may want to consider for their children. As a former Language Arts teacher and parent myself, I am always on the lookout for great books to purchase for my own 8th grade daughter. I also rely on my friends here in other content areas to keep me up to speed on possible gifts related to other school subjects. Here are a few suggestions I received from our resident language arts experts that I wanted to pass along to any parents in search of holiday gift ideas:

From Mrs. Chalk:

Ruby Holler by Sharon Creech
Measle and the Wrathmonk by Ian Ogilvy (if you like Harry Potter, this is the book for you!)
Looking for Bobowicz by Daniel Pinkwater
When Ratboy Lived Next Door by Chris Woodworth

From Mrs. Hopkins:

Joey Pigza Swallowed the Key, What Would Joey Do? I Am Not Joey Pigza Jack Gantos
Hoot, Flush Carl Hiaasen
What Do Fish Have To Do With Anything? And Other Stories Avi
Leaping Beauty and Other Animal Fairy Tales Gregory Maguire
Dogsong Gary Paulsen
Shark Girl Kelly Bingham

From Mrs. Prothro:

Among the Hidden by Margaret Peterson Haddix
Wayside School Gets a Little Stranger by Louis Sachar
Sideways Stories from Wayside School by Louis Sachar
Anne Frank: Beyond the Diary by Van Der Rol (I personally really love this book)
Birchbark House by Louise Erdrich

From Mrs. Richardson:

True stories of miraculous events: (Kids and adults love these!)
Angel Dogs by Allen and Linda Anderson
Angel Cats by Allen and Linda Anderson
Horse Miracles by Brad Steiger and Sherry Hansen Steiger
Small Miracles: Extraordinary Coincidences from Every-day Life by Yitta Halberstam and Judith Leventhal (One of my absolute favorites!)

A Must for Teens: (I bought all for my own daughter)
The 7 Habit of Highly Effective Teens by Sean Covey
Life Strategies for Teens by Jay McGraw
Rich Dad Poor Dad for Teens: The Secrets About Money That You Don't Learn In School by Robert Kiyosaki and Sharon Lechter

Fiction:
The Mysterious Benedict Society by Trenton Lee Stewart and Carson Ellis (Great for gifted kids!)
Shark Girl by Kelly Bingham (This author is coming to visit us in February and students will get to attend a special reception and have their books autographed if they have purchased and read her book.)
Jeremy Fink and the Meaning of Life by Wendy Mass
Maximum Ride by James Patterson
Uglies by Scott Westerfeld
Specials by Scott Westerfeld
Pretties by Scott Westerfeld
Stormbreaker by Anthony Horowitz
Ark Angel by Anthony Horowitz
Scorpia by Anthony Horowitz

In addition to the above, our Media Specialist, Mrs. Perkins, has compiled an extensive list of great books; see the Media Center News for her suggestions. I hope that you will find some enticing gift possibilities within the list above; teachers, thanks for these ideas!

Again, although our remaining school days on the 2007 calendar are limited, the tasks before us are important and the activities that await us are numerous. Please consult your calendars and heed the daily announcements so that you do not miss out on our basketball games, concerts, dances, and club meetings and events. Also, please keep in mind that the final week of this semester (December 17–21) will be extremely important, as students will be taking end of semester exams for all classes on some or all of these days. I wish you all the most joyous of holiday seasons!

Sincerely,

Jeff Zoul
Principal

Much like every idea relating to communication that we have discussed in this chapter, a key component of the school newsletter is consistency. If it is distributed each month at the same time to all stakeholders, with a consistent organization in terms of content and style, recipients will come to anticipate the school newsletter as a way to keep abreast of school events and school performance. The monthly letter written by the principal is vital in setting the tone for the school letter. In addition to communicating core factors, points of emphasis, and reasons for celebration in each newsletter, the principal may want to include seasonal aspects as well. In the letter above, Jeff shares teacher suggestions for parents looking to buy books for their children as gifts. Parents look forward to receiving these suggestions, teachers enjoy offering their expertise in this area, and the school communicates that the holiday gift-giving season and essential academic skills, such as reading, can be interrelated.

Clarifying the C.O.R.E.: Communication

As we stated at the outset of this book, the four dimensions of teaching, learning, and leading that we both value above all others and that pervade all areas of the school, ultimately impacting its climate, culture, teacher morale, and student academic achievement, are *Communication*, *Observation*, *Relationships*, and *Expectations*. Educators committed to making a difference in the lives of students, each other, and the school itself must plan for excelling in each of these areas. Although most would agree that effective communication between and among all stakeholders is critical to the success of any organization, it is not always the case that such communication practices exist. Too often, we take for granted that others within the organization share our sense of purpose, our values, and our goals. As teachers and leaders, we must strategically plan and implement communication vehicles that inform, solicit input, and build trust.

Our purpose in the previous section of this chapter has simply been to offer a few simple, yet specific, strategies that educators can adopt to communicate effectively and consistently. We have witnessed firsthand all of these communication tools carried out successfully and making a difference at several schools in which we have worked. Although these ideas are helpful ways for educators to communicate and can be immediately implemented at any school, they remain subordinate in importance to an even more vital component of communication: our daily informal interactions with our students, our parents, our community members, and each other. What and how we communicate through these daily interactions is of monumental importance. Teachers and administrators must communicate with parents, each other, and—most importantly—students in a dignified and respectful manner. As Todd has suggested on countless occasions, we must do this ten days out of ten, not just most of the time. In both our school-wide vehicles for formal communication and our daily interpersonal communications, we must also communicate with *confidence, consistency,* and *courage.*

Ultimately, the success or failure of any school is directly attributable to the actions of the educators working within the school. We are the variables who have the power to script much of what occurs each day. To be successful, we must communicate with confidence what we are doing, why we are doing it, and what we need others to do to support our efforts. We must stand confidently in this regard, acting from what Rick Smith (2004) calls a sense of inner authority. Whether we are teachers or administrators, we can never have too much inner authority in our communications with students, parents, and each other. Acting and communicating with confidence and inner authority "facilitates calm and harmony" (Smith, 2004, p. 23) and imparts to those within the school community a sense that classrooms and the school overall are being driven purposefully and are being led by educators who are capable and secure in their knowledge of what must be accomplished and how best to accomplish it. Confident educators are not cocky or arrogant, but they are unflappable in their quest to communicate clearly their expectations and take communicative actions to ensure these expectations are being met on a daily basis. Whether a situation calls for a teacher to place a phone call to a difficult parent regarding their child's behavior or for an administrator to conference with an underperforming teacher, the educator in the position of authority must communicate with *confidence*.

One way that educators can enhance their ability to communicate with confidence is through consistency. Many of the communication strategies discussed previously in this chapter succeed in part because they are actions that are carried out on an almost rigidly consistent basis. Returning to the example of dealing with a difficult parent or communicating with an underperforming teacher, consistency is of paramount importance. Simply establishing clear expectations is not enough; we must also consistently communicate how others are progressing in meeting these expectations. We must firmly, fairly, and consistently communicate with those who are not meeting our expectations, whether we are working with students, parents, or each other. We must also consistently communicate to those who are performing at or above expectations. The more consistently we communicate, the more confident we become in our abilities to help our schools succeed. In order to communicate effectively, we must communicate *consistently*.

At times, communicating honestly requires courage. We have yet to meet the successful teacher or administrator who actually enjoys communicating unhappy news. Yet, we have met thousands of educators who do so confidently, consistently, and effectively. They possess the courage—derived from their convictions—necessary to confront the brutal facts (Collins, 2001) that must be addressed if schools are to succeed. They also possess the courage to say simple, but powerful, phrases such as, "I don't know" or "I'm sorry" or "I need help with that; you're better at that than I am" or "I made a mistake" whenever the situation calls for it. Courageous communication requires that educators share authority and work collaboratively. It requires that they hold each other accountable for carrying out the school's mission and values. Although not always comfortable, courageous communication results in trust among all stakeholders and a sense that the school is operating from a sense of moral purpose in moving forward to ensure success. Educators desiring to make a difference in student and school performance must communicate with courage.

Communication is of vital importance in our lives as educators. Collectively, educators within the school must establish clearly stated expectations for communicating with students, parents, and each other. The school must create vehicles for regularly communicating with stakeholders our mission, our values, and our progress. Educators must also communicate these beliefs through daily actions and interactions that are aligned with more formal communication vehicles. In both instances, we must practice communicating confidently, consistently, and courageously. Committed educators are masters of communicating their vision, their values, and their passion for what they do. They clarify the core value of communication at the outset of the year and act in strategic ways to embody this value throughout the school year to ensure optimal performance of all with whom they work.

Chapter Three

Observation: Strategies for Success

In the previous chapter, we emphasized the importance of communication with all stakeholders regarding everything that occurs within the school. Of course, we cannot communicate about what is taking place in our schools, in our classrooms, and in our community that impacts learning unless we strategically and consciously observe these activities. At first glance, the word "observation" aligned with a book about education might bring to mind simply the traditional observations that school administrators schedule to evaluate classroom teachers. Although this is indeed a component of our core value, observation in the school setting should encompass a great deal more. It is certainly true that administrators should observe teachers teaching (although such observations should occur much more often than they do at most schools we have visited and should be conducted for a wide variety of purposes, not merely evaluation), yet teachers should also observe each other, and all educators must carefully observe their students. We must also pay close attention to our school facility to see what it implies about our beliefs and actions. We should observe our school community and track changes in growth and demographics. We should observe educators at other schools in our area and around the nation, when possible, searching out and learning from pockets of excellence we find around us. We should observe what occurs on our school buses periodically and even observe our students engaged in extracurricular

Facets of Observation			
The act of noticing, perceiving, regarding attentively, and the information secured by such acts.			
Educators effective in the core skill of observation:			
♦ Acknowledge	♦ Evaluate	♦ Intuit	♦ Reflect
♦ Analyze	♦ Examine	♦ Measure	♦ Research
♦ Ascertain	♦ Focus	♦ Monitor	♦ See
♦ Attend	♦ Follow Up	♦ Notice	♦ Study
♦ Check	♦ Infer	♦ Perceive	♦ Supervise
♦ Contemplate	♦ Inspect	♦ Probe	♦ Survey
♦ Detect	♦ Interpret	♦ Record	♦ View

activities. Educators focused on and skilled in the area of observation recognize the multiple facets of observation and purposefully plan for fulfilling all components of this core responsibility outlined below in a systematic, consistent manner.

Effective Observation Defined

When we refer to "observation" we actually use this term to include all facets listed above. In essence, we are firm believers that teachers and administrators must strategically, regularly, and consistently observe students learning and teachers teaching. The word most closely associated with "observation" that we consider a critical component of this core value is "monitor." We must monitor what occurs in every area of our school—but most importantly, of course, in our classrooms. Teachers and administrators must monitor, for example, that the intended curriculum becomes the taught curriculum. Then, we must monitor our assessment practices to ensure that the taught curriculum aligns with the one that we assess. Finally, we must use these assessment results to drive future actions.

Reeves (2006) suggests that it is not enough to merely plan for improvement in student achievement; we must also monitor these plans. That is, we must regularly observe the results we receive in terms of all types of data and adjust our actions accordingly. Schmoker (2006) writes that we must have the courage to monitor the curriculum, with teachers and administrators meeting together regularly to demonstrate that we are teaching the agreed-upon standards and ensuring that progress is being made toward improvement goals with ongoing assessments and adjustments to instruction based upon analysis of these assessment results. Of the 21 leadership responsibilities that impact student academic achievement according to Marzano, Waters, and McNulty (2005), that of monitoring and evaluation—monitoring "the effectiveness of school practices and their impact on student learning" (p. 43)—was associated with immediate and sustained change.

While observing what is occurring in classrooms and monitoring the implementation of the curriculum as well as the results we are achieving is of utmost importance, it is also important that we observe the physical presentation of our school. In his article, "The Schoolhouse at Midnight," Hoerr (2005/06) lightheartedly describes leading aliens on a late night tour of a school. He shrewdly suggests that our schoolhouse halls and walls are prime opportunities for broadcasting school values both to internal and external audiences. The subtle messages we send through the decorations, colors, words, and student work we have posted serve as powerful messages and can communicate a positive or negative learning environment. Displays of student work can serve as the most powerful learning signs we observe in schools. As Hoerr points out, however, it is not enough to merely post student work, we must accompany each piece with an explanation of the purpose of the work, how it connects to our curriculum, and why it was chosen for display. Although rounding up aliens to accompany us may prove difficult, we strongly encourage every teacher and administrator—regardless of how long they have served at their current school—to conduct such a walk around the entire campus, observing and recording what they see and what that says about the school and its core values. Observing our students learning and our teachers teaching is of obvious and foremost importance. Yet, it is hugely important that we carefully observe the physical appearance of all aspects of our campus—from the parking lots to the lunchroom to the hallway walls—to discern what we are communicating about our school through these outward messages.

Our core value of observation is closely associated with a multitude of other educator responsibilities, including that of communication, described in Chapter One, in that we must communicate with others what it is we are observing. We define the act of observation as educators who are visible, who are aware, and who monitor and adjust to what it is they notice and see in every classroom, throughout the school campus, and within the school community. The more visible educators are, the more aware they are of how the school is performing. The more aware educators are, the better able they are to monitor progress and adjust their practices accordingly in order to achieve desired results. What follows are just a few ways teachers and school leaders can employ specific observation strategies to improve student and school performance. The strategies we have outlined below require very little of the practitioner, other than a commitment to move from knowing they are important to actually following through and implementing them at their schools. Each suggestion below is rather simple to understand and implement and can be used at the elementary, middle, or high school level. In addition, we offer ideas for teachers and administrators, as well as ideas that pertain to both groups of educators.

Peer Observations

While it is important—and presumably mandatory—that administrators conduct observations of all classroom teachers for the purpose of monitoring and evaluation, we strongly encourage school leaders to also establish a formal or informal process allowing for peer observations, so that teachers can observe each other in the act of teaching students. Peer observations can be used as part of an induction and/or mentoring process, as a way to recognize superstar teachers who may have much to offer colleagues who observe them teaching, and even as part of the supervision process. Hoerr (2006/2007) suggests that involving our superstar teachers in peer observations can yield powerful benefits for both star teachers and emerging stars. Who better to offer ideas to teachers struggling with an issue than another teacher who has faced and overcome the same or similar obstacle? Ellis, Smith, and Abbot (1979) even found that peer observations can help the supervision process, reporting that teachers who were observed by peers as well as supervisors had significantly improved attitudes toward the supervision process. In our own experience, we have found a somewhat surprising additional benefit to the peer observation program: our veteran superstar teachers love—and learn a great deal from—observing first-year teachers. Often, these new teachers arrive at the teaching profession with new ideas that our superstar teachers are excited to try once they see them in action firsthand. We have long argued that there should be no pecking order in schools. Superior performance today trumps years of repetitive, mediocre experience and while it is often the case that new teachers can benefit from observing our veterans, it is equally true that our veteran teachers can and should learn from new teachers.

Establishing a peer observation process in any school is relatively easy. Schools may want to require that each teacher observe another teacher once each month. Administrators may want to periodically cover classes for teachers who are observing a colleague. Peer observations can be brief, perhaps 15–20 minutes, and a simple reporting form can be used, with copies given to the teacher being observed as well as an administrator or department leader. In school districts that have elementary, middle, and high schools included, principals may opt to have teachers at their school conduct one of their observation reports at the school that feeds into them or the school into which they feed. Typically, the partner school is thrilled that teachers from a feeder school want to learn more about what is occurring in their own classrooms. On the following page is a sample form we have used in implementing a peer observation program, calling the visits "OMS Reports," an acronym both for the school name and for the idea of **O**bserving **M**asterful **S**taff.

Focused Classroom Walks

In addition to asking individual teachers to observe several of their colleagues while engaged in teaching lessons, we have also found it useful for teachers and administrators to conduct small-group focused classroom walks. In such focused observations, typically a small group (ideally between three and six) of educators visit a teacher's classroom for a group observation. At times, the group is comprised simply of several teachers from the same building. On the other hand, schools may choose to have an administrator included in the group or even teachers from neighboring schools and/or staff from the district office. When conducting focused classroom walks, we again suggest that visits last no more than 15–20 minutes. In addition, rather

Otwell Middle School
Observing Masterful Staff
Reporting Form

Observing Teacher: _____

Name of Teacher Being Observed: _____

Date: _____ Time: _____

Grade Level/Subject: _____

Description of Teaching and Learning Activities: _____

_____

_____

_____

_____

_____

_____

_____

_____

Wows! and Wonders: _____

_____

_____

_____

_____

_____

_____

_____

_____

_____

than merely observing all that is occurring within the classroom, we suggest using these opportunities to focus on only one or two specific areas of teaching and learning. Ideally, these focused observation points of emphasis are established in a pre-conference held with the teacher being observed and the focused walk team prior to the observation itself. It may be that a teacher wants the team to focus on anything the teacher does related to classroom management, questioning techniques, student and teacher movement, the level of student engagement, or the quality of work assigned and completed.

Once the team of teachers is organized and has met with the teacher being observed to set the focus of the visit, team members visit the classroom, talking with students quietly and observing and noting anything they see related to the agreed-upon focus of the observation. Afterwards, the team should meet with the teacher to share what they noted individually and what themes appeared to emerge collectively. A variation on this idea that may be done across grade levels or academic departments is to set a focus area for the entire team, grade level, or department rather than an individual teacher. Then, teams of observers can take turns visiting all teachers within the group to focus on one or two key areas of instruction vital to all members of the group. After all team members have been observed, the large group can meet together to hold an extensive conversation about what they observed in a variety of rooms while focusing on a sole area of instruction. It is important to note that this process should be non-evaluative; instead, this is intended to be a learning experience for all involved, both the team of observers and the teachers being observed.

Conducted on a school-wide level, focused classroom walks can be a powerful way to observe firsthand what we are doing in classrooms throughout the building in terms of specific areas of instruction. At many schools we are familiar with, the post-observation conversations have provided rich dialogue among educators in which teachers openly and genuinely learned from and shared with each other. As with most ideas worth pursuing in our noble profession, finding the time to conduct such walks and host follow-up conferences analyzing such visits requires time. Administrators may need to explore creative ways to provide release time for teachers so that periodic focused classroom walks can be successfully accomplished. In our experiences at all grade levels, the investment in such efforts pays huge dividends. In fact, we have seen focused classroom walks woven into school improvement plans and as an integral part of a school's new teacher induction program. Any time we can get educators to observe each other teaching is likely to benefit both the teacher as well as the teacher-observer.

Visibility

The most effective and efficient way for educators to fulfill our core value of observation is simply by remaining highly visible throughout the school. For the school principal, visibility "...addresses the extent to which the school leader has contact and interacts with teachers, students, and parents" (Marzano, Waters, & McNulty, 2005, p. 61). Yet, teachers should be equally visible throughout the school and beyond: in the hallways, in the cafeteria, in each other's classrooms, on the playground, and at extracurricular events. By remaining highly visible throughout the school and at all school events, teachers and administrators not only communicate to others that they care about all that occurs relating to the school, but also have unlimited opportunities to interact with each other and observe how the students and the school are performing. In terms of administrator visibility in classrooms, we feel that 30 observations in a teacher's classroom for five minutes each over the course of a school year yields much more information about teachers and their students than a formal observation of 45 minutes once or twice per year. As for teachers, those who are consistently visible in the hallways, observing all that occurs, not only provide for a more safe and orderly learning environment, but also are able to interact informally with the students they teach, connecting with them in ways that can pay dividends back in the classroom.

Not surprisingly, the obstacle of "not enough time" often rears its ugly head once again as an impediment to teachers and administrators being more visible in the ways described above. Teachers are too busy preparing for the next class to step into the hall to supervise and interact with kids; principals are too busy with various tasks that seem to chain them to their offices. We again maintain that overcoming such obstacles is a matter of priority and that being highly visible should stand as a core priority for every educator working in a school. School administrators should set a goal of conducting brief observations in a certain number of classrooms each day and should prioritize these visits by conducting them at the outset of the day before impending crises have a chance to interfere with this commitment. In addition, as principals we both made it a regular practice to complete any administrative task that could be accomplished away from our offices inside classrooms, working on our work alongside students who were working on theirs. Students not only seemed to enjoy seeing us working in their classrooms, they tended to behave better when we were present as well. For many years, Todd has maintained that there is very little administrators can do in their offices while school is in session that has a direct and immediate impact on school improvement. Instead, to improve the school, the principal needs to be where the action is: the classrooms, the hallways, the cafeterias, the playgrounds—wherever students and teachers are gathered.

Teachers, too, can make a huge difference in the lives of students and the school overall simply by "being there." All teachers know that they should monitor hallways during transition times, and all teachers know that they should be visible at extracurricular events from time to time. Great teachers follow through on this knowledge and act upon it, while mediocre teachers focus only on what occurs within the four walls of their classroom. In our experience, we have found that teachers who already have the most job-related commitments are the ones who somehow find the time to also attend an after-school event or eat lunch with a student, or monitor the halls on a consistent basis. Our mediocre teachers are too busy complaining or making excuses to do either. Ultimately, of course, this investment of time on the part of our superstar teachers pays off; as students recognize this adult presence and commitment, their respect for such dedication increases and their behavior for such teachers improves. Jeff served as principal at one school with a widely recognized teacher of the year, Ronnie McNeese. Mr. McNeese is not only one of the best math teachers we have ever known, he is also a valued member of the school's leadership team and a successful football and basketball coach. After a particularly grueling week of teaching and coaching, Ronnie was second-guessing his promise to attend a performance of *The Nutcracker*, in which one of his 6th grade students was participating. He was even more despondent when he arrived and learned that it was a ballet! Yet, this investment of time—although a huge personal sacrifice—made an equally huge impression on this young student and her family, who were amazed that their daughter's math teacher and the school's football coach took the time to attend a ballet performance on a Friday night. Imagine the impact Ronnie's presence at this event had on his relationship with this student and her family the rest of the school year.

Serving as a highly visible teacher or administrator is both one of the easiest and hardest things we can do to positively impact our schools. On the one hand, it requires very little brain power, paperwork, planning time, or creativity. On the other hand, daily obstacles, crises, time constraints, and unplanned interruptions to our busy schedules often intervene to prevent us from fulfilling this core responsibility. Although these obstacles arise at every school and face every educator, great schools are filled with educators who still find a way to remain highly visible on a consistent basis. Schools staffed with such dedicated educators benefit from this level of visibility. As Hall (2005, p. 13) noted, "Visibility breeds reassurance and familiarity, while at the same time offering a healthy dose of fear and order." Students want to see their teachers throughout the school and our best teachers want to see their administrators in their classrooms and throughout the school. In addition, our mediocre teachers may be less comfortable with such a strong administrative presence. Since they are aware that they may be observed at any given time, they may work harder to improve their instructional practices. A strong visible presence on the part of teachers and administrators results in a more orderly and positive learning environment.

Arrival and Departure

A specific way to accomplish the goal of learning more about what is occurring at our schools through visibility is by consistently greeting students at the beginning and the end of each school day. These are critical times of the day, which can set the tone for the learning that is about to take place as well as the learning just concluded. With 180 days in a school year, we have 360 chances during the course of the year to observe our kids arriving to or departing from our schools. We can learn a great deal from these observations, proactively deflecting potential problems, enhancing learning that has or will occur, ensuring a safe and orderly learning environment, and interacting with our students and with each other. A key to succeeding in positively impacting the school in this way is consistency. One principal we know has established at his school a goal that each child receives a warm greeting from three caring adults before they even enter a classroom. We must commit to being there as our kids arrive and depart 360 times out of 360 opportunities.

As students arrive to school each day, we suggest having at least one administrator and perhaps a teacher stationed at the area where students arrive by car or foot, as well as the bus arrival area. Make it a goal to verbally greet and shake the hand of every student as they enter the school, telling them to have a great day, asking how the weekend was, or pulling them aside and encouraging them to make good choices that day. In addition to greeting each student, we can also observe them carefully as they arrive and address any potential concerns we might detect. This is a good time, for instance, to immediately address any dress code issues, before students have even stepped into a classroom. In addition, we might notice that a student who we know to be struggling is arriving without a book bag or any school materials. We can immediately pull them aside and talk about completing work at home and coming to school prepared.

At the close of each day, we should do the same, monitoring our kids as they exit the school, wishing each a good afternoon and again holding brief conversations with students who may need a reminder about behavioral or academic expectations or just a special word of support. We have found that connecting with students in this way on a consistent basis makes a difference in their attitude and performance. Students who know us and know that we will be there each morning and afternoon watching them and greeting them tend to respect our presence and our friendly supervision. Even our most reluctant learners or most ill-behaved students tend to try harder to do the right thing when they know we are there, watching them and speaking to them as they come and go each and every day.

In addition to positioning teachers and administrators outside to greet students as they arrive and depart, it is extremely beneficial to have staff members stationed in various common areas and hallways as students proceed to their classrooms in the morning or the exits in the afternoon. Finally, we complete the morning and afternoon observation coverage by having every teacher stationed outside their classrooms, observing their individual students and greeting them accordingly. A smile and a word of encouragement from the teacher here can significantly impact what is about to occur within the classroom. Teachers who might suggest that they are too busy doing last minute planning to stand in the halls fail to realize that this form of observation is an even more important component of planning. As we observe students entering our room, we are making observations about their appearance, their attitude, their countenance, their level of preparedness, and their energy and enthusiasm—all things we must take into consideration as we plan for subsequent learning.

Even at our most affluent schools, we seem to have a surprising number of students who come to us from less than ideal home lives. For years, Todd has shared his personal goal to create school cultures in which it is "cool to care" (Whitaker, 2004, p. 115). By committing to stationing ourselves in places where we can greet our kids at the beginning and the close of each school day, we are showing that we care about our students, many of whom count on us as much as they do their own family to provide them this feeling of being cared for. While we make our kids' lives just a little bit better each day with this small sign of personalized care, we, too, are benefiting from this practice, in that these same students are more likely to learn and work according to our level of expectation because we care.

Meeting Locations

Many schools are large enough that the only feasible location to host a whole faculty meeting is the auditorium, cafeteria, or media center. Whenever possible, however, we like to hold faculty meetings in classrooms throughout the building. Barth (1990) suggests this as a way to force teachers who had previously isolated themselves within their own classrooms into those of their colleagues. He even suggests having the teacher who is "hosting" the faculty meeting start it off by sharing a little bit about their classroom and any special strategies they use that are successful with students. Convening a meeting in a classroom as opposed to any other area of the school provides those in attendance a chance to observe a great deal about what occurs within that classroom.

At large schools with many teachers on staff, it may be impossible to convene all teachers in one classroom at the same time for a faculty meeting. Still, it is important that any meeting that can be held in a classroom, including department meetings, professional learning community meetings, SST meetings, and IEP meetings, be held there as opposed to an office or commons area. The classroom is where our core business occurs, and we can observe and learn more about our school—even when students are not present—by being in classrooms. When teachers meet regularly in small groups—such as department or grade-level meetings—we suggest following Barth's (1990) lead and arranging for teachers within these small groups to rotate the responsibility of hosting the meeting in their classrooms and starting off the meeting by sharing one specific idea that is working for them in the classroom. It is also helpful to convene all parent meetings in classrooms rather than in offices. Parents can observe firsthand where their children learn each day, and teachers have at their fingertips materials relating to the student's performance. We have even found that difficult parents have a harder time behaving in a difficult manner when we are meeting in a classroom as opposed to an office.

When faculty numbers are such that the entire faculty simply cannot meet in a single classroom at the same time, we still have found a way to meet in classrooms on a rotating basis. We call these our "carousel" meetings, and we often use this format on professional learning days. In carousel meetings, we assign teachers to groups of no more than 25, so with a staff of 100, for example, we would have four or five groups of teachers, depending on how many sessions we wanted to conduct. Each group rotates around to each session during the time allotted. For example, at the beginning of the school year, we might have four sessions, with the principal leading one and assistant principals, counselors, or teaching leaders conducting the others. The four topics might last for 30 minutes each and focus on school safety, staff expectations, differentiation, and standards-based unit design. Leaving five minutes in between each session for transition, over the course of just over two hours, each teacher on staff would learn about four different aspects of teaching and learning within the school and would do so while visiting the classrooms of four colleagues. We tend to group these classrooms close to one another, but vary them by hallway, department, or grade level each time we host carousel meetings. One day, we might meet in four different 8th grade classrooms; the next time we meet in such a manner, we might choose four different math classrooms in which to meet. Learning in classrooms throughout the building affords us the opportunity to observe what other classrooms look and feel like—and also provides us the unusual experience of placing ourselves in our students' shoes for a while as we sit in their seats learning. In our experiences conducting such meetings, we have often observed teachers not only learning the information being delivered, but also writing down ideas that they glean from glancing about a classroom that they are sitting in for the first time.

Visiting Other Schools

We recently had the opportunity to accompany several teachers on a day-long visit to the Ron Clark Academy in Atlanta, Georgia, a school of 60 students in grades 5 and 6. Clark is the nationally acclaimed teacher, speaker, and author, whose life as a teacher was recently chronicled in a popular television movie starring Matthew Perry. After their visit to the Ron Clark Academy, two teachers we were working with returned to their school energized, enthused, and transformed, leading the rest of the faculty in a re-delivery of what they had observed and what parts of that could be replicated at their own school. They even conducted an enormously successful academic decathlon on the final day of the semester, basing their idea on something they had observed while visiting this school. The academic decathlon proved to be one of the most successful events of the entire school year, with students and teachers actively engaged in the curriculum while having a great deal of fun.

Admittedly, the Ron Clark Academy is a very unusual school and much of what is in place there (including a two-story slide utilized by students and teachers traveling from the second to first floor!) cannot easily be implemented at other schools. However, the overall climate and culture of the school is one that can serve as a model for any other school. Characteristics in place at the Ron Clark Academy, such as enthusiasm, creativity, positive energy, strict discipline, dignity and respect for all, and engaging lessons, are ones that are transferable to any school staffed with teachers willing to observe schools committed to such a culture and change their professional practices to cultivate equally positive school cultures. Moreover, one need not visit the amazing Ron Clark Academy to be so inspired. The truth is, we can learn a great deal from a visit to any school and—regardless of where we live—there are many nearby from which we can learn. At times, we may learn what *not* to do, but more often we will find something being done in another school that sparks our interest or imagination as something that we would like to try at our own school in order to improve our practices.

Neighboring schools are a rich—and often untapped—resource for observing teaching and learning in a different environment from the one to which we become so accustomed. We encourage administrators and teachers to use observations at other schools as a portion of their annual professional growth plan. Commit at least one day each year to visiting a school with the goal of observing as much as possible and returning with at least a handful of ideas to share with others at your school. Although we are strong believers that the most powerful professional learning that occurs at a school oftentimes emanates from within the school itself, observing teaching and learning at other schools is an extremely practical way to see what is working elsewhere.

In addition to visiting other schools in an effort to learn new and effective ways to improve instruction, we can also learn by returning the favor and inviting educators from other schools to observe our own. As principals, we regularly hosted visiting teachers and administrators who had heard about something good that was occurring at our schools and wanted to see for themselves how we were doing it. Inevitably during these visits, the teachers who were doing the observing would exchange some of their own ideas from their schools that were also working and we would learn from them, too. Educators who want to make a difference can learn a great deal from each other. We have worked at many schools in which educators have truly broken down the barriers of isolation within, encouraging teachers to observe and learn from each other. Observing and learning from teachers and administrators at neighboring schools is less common and a valuable potential resource for new ideas. We encourage all educators to set a goal of visiting at least one school other than their own for one day each year; the learning gained will be well worth the effort.

Student Teachers

When hiring teachers, we believe it is important to let prospective candidates know that once hired, we want the other teachers at the school to become more like the new teacher rather than the other way around. This strikes most veteran educators as counterintuitive at first glance, and we certainly realize that any new teacher has much to learn about our profession, our school system, and our individual school. Yet, our point is that we aim to hire new teachers to our school who are so outstanding in one or more areas that they will be able to share their wisdom in those areas with even our most veteran and expert teachers already on board. Along these same lines, we are staunch advocates for welcoming as many student teachers to work in our schools as possible. Colleges and universities are always trying to place education majors in schools either for full time internships or part time field experiences. Administrators and teachers should make every effort to invite these future teachers to their schools and classrooms, observing—and learning from—them as they find their way as a teacher, presumably trying out new ideas and strategies with which we may be unfamiliar and can then consider. Working with student teachers can certainly be an added burden to an already-busy classroom teacher, and some interns will be more successful than others, but we have found it decidedly advantageous to reach out to these future educators, helping and teaching them how to be effective and learning as much as possible from them in return.

Having student teachers in the building promotes an overall school culture of continuous learning and fosters a sense of collaboration. We often ask our administrators and teacher leaders to observe these practicing teachers once they begin teaching lessons as part of their internship. In addition, we always ask our student teachers to conduct several 30-minute observations of our best teachers. Having student teachers in the school is just one more way for educators to observe each other in action, inevitably learning and helping each other along the way. In addition to the benefits of having student teachers in classrooms for the purposes of observation, learning, mentoring, and collaboration, an added benefit, of course, is that schools who actively recruit student teachers hold an inside edge on hiring the very best among them once teaching openings arise.

Teacher Observations/Evaluations

One thing can safely be said about the teacher evaluation process: if a perfect system existed for evaluating our teachers effectively, efficiently, consistently, and fairly, we would all be using such a system. Instead, school systems around the country have struggled with finding an effective way to observe teachers and evaluate their performance. Like many aspects of education, it seems as if the pendulum has swung back and forth a few times, from trying to completely standardize the process using rigid forms and other "objective" tools, to open-ended approaches with teachers preparing portfolios as evidence of what they have accomplished throughout the year. Presumably, the guidelines in place for evaluating teachers at any school emanate from the school system's central office. The task of each school is for teachers and administrators to work together to use whatever district guidelines are in place to best optimize the performance of teachers—and, ultimately, students. As we stated at the outset, no perfect process for accomplishing this currently exists. Not surprisingly, we are not prepared or equipped to share the perfect solution within these pages, either. However, we do know this: *observing* and *monitoring* the actions that both teachers and students engage in and the results that both teachers and students achieve should be the focus of this process as opposed to *evaluating* their performance. If administrators observe and monitor teachers and students in the classroom on a regular basis, the evaluation process unfolds naturally. The more we observe and monitor instruction, the more comfortable teachers are with such a presence and a greater likelihood exists that real change will occur as compared to traditional models wherein an administrator might make an annual appearance in the classroom and subsequently judge the performance of the teacher based on this sole observation. In observing, monitoring, and evaluating teachers, we suggest that teachers and administrators begin by establishing clear guidelines for how this process will evidence itself throughout the year. Again, until the perfect teacher evaluation framework is discovered, this process will continue to vary from school to school, but we suggest that the following components should play a critical role in any teacher evaluation/development process:

(1) *Know what to look for.* At the outset of each new year, school administrators should make it explicitly clear what the school-wide goals for improvement are, based on past performance. As soon as possible once the school year commences, administrators should meet with individual teachers or small groups of teachers to agree on what goals they might have specific to their content area or grade level. Once these overarching goals and more specific goals are discerned and agreed to, the focus of future observations and monitoring efforts must center on these areas. How are teachers advancing the goals of the school's continuous improvement process and their own goals for improving academic achievement of the students they teach?

(2) *Lead with questions.* When observing in classrooms, administrators should focus more on what students are learning as opposed to what the teacher is teaching. Look for answers to questions such as: What is the goal of the lesson and are the students clear about this? Are the students aware of what it is they are expected to know and be able to do as an outcome of the lesson? What are the students engaged in doing and what is their level of engagement? How will the teacher assess student learning of the intended outcomes? In addition to looking for answers to these questions and others during the observation itself, administrators and teachers should hold conversations about these as they meet together to plan, implement, and monitor instruction.

(3) *Focus on results.* At its essence, our core business is, of course, student learning. In observing and evaluating teachers then, we must focus on the results they are achieving related to student learning. In doing so, we must be honest, focus on the positive, and clearly and openly address areas of underperformance, without casting blame or making excuses.

(4) *Acknowledge the variable.* We are firm believers that the teacher is the primary variable in terms of student learning. We fully realize that students come in all shapes and sizes with wide-ranging family backgrounds and learning strengths and challenges, yet we feel that teachers have the power—and responsibility—to effect dramatic growth in all students. Although student demographic characteristics definitely have a relationship to student learning, we believe that superior teaching trumps challenging student demographics. The focus should not necessarily be on showing that all students in a teacher's class exceeded standards; instead, the focus must be on student growth, as evidenced by gains in academic achievement throughout the year. To paraphrase a long-standing saying, where our students end up is not nearly as important as how far they advanced from whence they began. Even our superstar teachers cannot move every student to valedictorian status, but we should expect all teachers to close achievement gaps where they exist, with documented gains in achievement for all students. We cannot allow each other to accept excuses for lack of learning; we must acknowledge that we, as educators, are the most important variable relating to student achievement.

(5) *Provide support.* A key component to any plan for observing, supervising, and evaluating staff is providing support. Perhaps more so in education than any other career field, people choose our profession for noble reasons; most educators would state that they chose this particular career because they wanted to make a difference in the lives of young people. Educators tend to be motivated and driven by a sense of purpose and meaning rather than by financial incentives. We say this to suggest that in a great majority of cases, our underperforming teachers are not horrible people, displaying a poor work ethic, a lack of integrity, or an unwillingness to improve. Presumably, a few such educators do exist, but the vast majority of our struggling teachers are professionals

who want to improve and are willing to accept our support. It is one of our foremost responsibilities as administrators and teacher leaders to provide it for them. Providing support for struggling teachers is a book in itself, beyond the scope of our purpose here, but our basic framework for assisting teachers who need our help is as follows: first, we must observe firsthand the teacher on more than one occasion. We must confer with the teacher to pinpoint areas of concern, remaining positive, yet honestly confronting the facts as we have observed them. Next, we must build trusting relationships with such teachers so that it is easier for them to agree when a problem exists that needs attention. Finally, we must enact a plan of support and follow up on this plan regularly, monitoring progress at several points throughout the school year. Of course, the specific plan for support is the key to improvement and will vary depending on the difficulty the teacher is experiencing, but many times it involves working with and observing colleagues who have faced similar obstacles and overcome them. Again, with a very small percentage of our underperforming teachers, our aim is, quite frankly, different. Rather than providing the support they need to improve, we are encouraging them to find a more suitable career. But for most situations involving teachers who are underperforming, we must do our best to help struggling teachers grow and improve as much as we can. They need unwavering support in this growth and development. Administrators and teacher leaders must make providing such support an urgent priority.

School Improvement Plans

Typically, when we exhort educators to focus on our core value of observation, we are speaking of observing human interactions, whether that means administrators observing teachers, teachers observing each other, or any educator observing students. However, it is also of vital importance that we observe the results we are achieving through our efforts. We must continuously monitor our student and teacher performance, observing what is having a positive impact on results they are achieving and what is not.

Reeves (2006) talks about the virtues of "ugly" plans as opposed to "pretty" plans. In essence, he is suggesting that too often, schools create continuous improvement plans at the outset of each new year, only to turn these in to the central office or store them away somewhere without ever revisiting, revising, or updating them. We find this to be a fatal flaw in many areas relating to education today, but it is particularly commonplace in the area of school improvement plans as well as teacher and administrator professional improvement plans. The plan itself should remain subordinate in importance to the implementation and monitoring of the plan. Thus, these plans should change during the course of the year, as we observe what kinds of results we are achieving along the way, fine tuning what is working, eliminating that which is not, and creating new ways to address what the data tells us needs our attention. As Reeves suggests, such malleable plans may turn "ugly" as the year progresses, but this is as it should be, as teachers and administrators work together to regularly examine student achievement.

At times, we will find that we have already achieved intended results and need to move beyond goals that have been set at the beginning of the year. At other times, we will find that we have fallen short of our expectations and that we must address how we will respond differently so that our goals can still be achieved. Oftentimes, we learn that certain groups of students are achieving at one end of the spectrum, exceeding expectations, while others have yet to master learning objectives. In these instances, we must adjust our plans, creating remediation interventions to close the achievement gap while providing enrichment opportunities for students who have mastered pre-established content objectives.

Schools that succeed do so not because of any plan they have written outlining how they will improve. Similarly, no educator improves his or her professional performance based on an individual plan for improvement they have crafted.

Instead, schools and individual educators only improve as they first work to implement such plans and then monitor their performance, changing the plans as appropriate. Successful educators avoid the trap of writing improvement plans at the beginning of the school year, only to place them aside and go about following their past practices regardless of what they observe in terms of student, teacher, and school performance.

Clarifying the C.O.R.E.: Observation

As we stated at the outset of this book, the four dimensions of teaching, learning, and leading which we both value above all others and which pervade all areas of the school, ultimately impacting its climate, culture, teacher morale, and student academic achievement are *Communication, Observation, Relationships,* and *Expectations*. Educators committed to making a difference in the lives of students, each other, and the school itself must plan for excelling in each of these core areas. Although most would agree that close scrutiny of every aspect of our schools through focused observation and monitoring is critical to its success, it is not always the case that such practices for observing how we are performing—and reacting accordingly—exist. Educators who want to positively impact the schools in which they serve must strategically and purposefully engage in activities which allow them to observe firsthand the actions, behaviors, attitudes, and performance levels of students, teachers, and administrators. Based on these observations, committed educators must act to improve in the aforementioned areas, continuously striving to achieve even greater results.

Our purpose in the previous section of this chapter has simply been to offer a few simple, but specific, strategies that educators can adopt to effectively and consistently observe how they are doing. We have witnessed firsthand all of these observation tools carried out successfully and making a difference at several schools in which we have worked. Weaving throughout all the above ideas relating to observation is the theme of "finding what one looks for." That is, we believe that educators—and people in general—typically find whatever it is they are looking for. If they are negative, pessimistic, and critical by nature, they will most assuredly find the world around them to be unpleasant, inadequate, unfair, and constantly in need of repair. Conversely, we often find in education overly positive professionals who see only the good in all situations and rarely focus in on what is not working and must be fixed. We have worked in schools in which highly educated, intelligent, and experienced educators have observed the exact same lesson or examined the exact same achievement data only to derive distinctly differing perspectives on the effectiveness of the lesson or the performance of the students. In sharing our views on observation within the realm of education, we like to encourage all educators to "find what they are looking for" but to make certain that they consciously look for specific things as they observe the operations of the school. In addition, educators should make an effort to observe both with a critical eye at times and with a favorable eye at others, looking for—and finding—areas in which there are obvious causes for celebrations while also purposefully looking for—and, ergo, finding—causes for concern. Rather than visiting classrooms and walking around the school merely seeing what is happening, we must focus on what we are looking for, varying this focus daily based on the needs of our students and our teachers. Armed with the belief that it is almost always possible to find what one is looking for, educators who want to make a difference should observe the teaching and learning occurring within the school consciously looking for both the good and the bad, or what we call, the *positive*, the *possible*, and the *positively unacceptable*.

In earlier works (Whitaker, 2003; Whitaker, 2004), Todd has maintained that great teachers and principals "raise the praise and minimize the criticize." That continues to be our primary focus as we observe in schools with an eye toward improving performance. One of our key responsibilities as teachers and administrators is to create positive learning environments, both in individual classrooms and throughout the school. As we observe our students and our teachers it is important to start by *looking for positives*. We must do this even when observing our mediocre teachers as well as our students who struggle most.

They may need this positive feedback even more than our superstar students and teachers before they can focus on improving those areas in which they are weak. Just as we innately build off the strengths of our own children as they begin to learn a new skill, so, too, must we focus on strengths and positive attributes of students and teachers in our schools who most need our help. Although praise and positive feedback are necessary starting points, we cannot, of course, shirk our responsibility of addressing underperformance and doing whatever necessary to improve the work of struggling students and teachers. Starting with a positive approach is the best way to effect change so that students, teachers, and schools succeed.

As we conduct various types of observations throughout our school, we must also do so with an eye toward *looking for the possible* rather than focusing on obstacles, time constraints, and other stumbling blocks to success. The more we observe all that is occurring within our schools, the more we discern what it is we need to do in order to improve them. Too often, we allow those inevitable obstacles which confront us all to interfere with the possibilities available for achieving our goals. At nearly all schools there are a certain percentage of students who fall behind, creating the infamous "achievement gap" so prevalent in education today. Certain schools seem to simply accept this gap as an inevitable result of socioeconomic status or other student demographics while other schools, faced with similar situations, seem to rise to the occasion of any challenge, planning, implementing, and monitoring programs designed to close such gaps. At one school where Todd served as principal, all teachers on staff unanimously agreed to extend the school day each day without pay in order to ensure that they had time to meet the learning needs of all students. At a school where Jeff served as principal, each teacher agreed to work for free two Saturday mornings each school year so that the school could remain open every Saturday from 9:00–12:00 staffed with five teachers and an administrator in an effort to hold all students accountable for completing every assignment. These are just two examples of dedicated educators, driven by core factors, looking for the possible—ways they could fix what they observed as problems currently occurring. Observing all that takes place at our schools with an eye toward imagining possibilities which would remedy that which we note as needing attention is another way to ensure school success.

Finally, it is an unpleasant reality that, periodically, all educators are faced with situations that are simply contrary to what we know is best for our schools. Successful educators observe all that occurs within the school, focusing on the positive and the possible regularly, but they also achieve results by *looking for the positively unacceptable* and confronting such situations fairly, firmly, and consistently. Every school we know of is filled with more good teachers who are well intentioned than subpar teachers. Likewise, every school we know of is filled with many more students who are well behaved and hardworking than the other way around. Although we both tend to focus on the positive as much as we can, we also know that we must look for unacceptable behaviors within our schools and take immediate steps to address them. Successful schools are filled with educators who work together to hold each other—and their students—accountable for remaining committed to the mission, vision, and values of the school. If unacceptable, counterproductive behavior is not addressed, one thing is certain: more such behavior will occur. Looking for and finding unacceptable situations within our schools is not nearly as fun as looking for and finding all the good that is occurring. Yet, it is equally important to the success of the school that administrators and teacher leaders have the courage and commitment to confront individuals acting in ways which are detrimental to student and teacher learning.

Observation is of vital importance in our lives as educators. Collectively, educators within the school must establish routines for observing students, each other, and all available school data. The school must consciously find what it is looking for, making sure to vary what it is looking for so that they see both what is working and what is not. Educators must observe daily actions and interactions which occur in all areas of the school, monitoring at regular intervals how they are progressing in terms of realizing stated goals. Committed educators are masters of observing learning in a way that is focused on improving performance. By looking for and finding the positive, the possible, and the positively unacceptable, they are upholding their responsibility to cultivate a school culture of inquiry, collaboration, and continuous improvement. Great educators clarify the core value of observation at the outset of the year and act in strategic ways to embody this value throughout the school year to ensure optimal performance of all with whom they work.

Chapter Four

Relationships: Strategies for Success

For years, Todd has written (Whitaker, 2003 & Whitaker, 2004) and spoken about his core belief that people, not programs, make the difference in schools. Programs—no matter how grand—are never the solution and they are never the problem. Rather, the people implementing such programs are always the problem and they are always the solution. While the people within any organization are clearly the key to that organization's success—or failure—it is not enough to simply have the right people in place. We agree with Fullan (2001) that *people are merely the starting place in the equation; it is the relationships* we cultivate and maintain between and among the people in our schools that make a significant impact on student and teacher performance. In today's schools, change is a constant. The relationships created in our schools during this era of seemingly continuous change must be grounded in trust and mutual respect in order for successful change to occur. According to Fullan (2001), "... the single factor common to every successful change initiative is that *relationships* improve. If relationships

---

Facets of Relationships

A particular type of connection or association which exists between people who have dealings with one another and who work to cultivate an awareness of each other's personal and professional lives.

Educators effective in the core skill of relationships:

♦ *Affect*	♦ *Identify With*	♦ *Regard*
♦ *Affiliate*	♦ *Influence*	♦ *Relate*
♦ *Affirm*	♦ *Inspire*	♦ *Sympathize*
♦ *Ally*	♦ *Interact*	♦ *Team Up*
♦ *Associate*	♦ *Involve*	♦ *Touch*
♦ *Band Together*	♦ *Join*	♦ *Tolerate*
♦ *Connect*	♦ *Link*	♦ *Transform*
♦ *Credit*	♦ *Move*	♦ *Understand*
♦ *Empathize*	♦ *Plug Into*	♦ *Unite*
♦ *Fit*	♦ *Recognize*	♦ *Verbalize*

improve, things get better. If they remain the same or get worse, ground is lost" (p. 5). As a result, all educators working within the school must consciously focus on building and maintaining positive relationships with students, with parents, with community members, and—most importantly—with each other. Educators focused on and skilled in the area of relationship building recognize the multiple facets of relationships and purposefully plan for fulfilling all components of this core responsibility outlined below in a systematic, consistent manner.

Effective Relationships Defined

If the three most important words in real estate are, "location, location, location," an equivalent in the realm of schools would be, "relationships, relationships, relationships." In every walk of life, forging strong and positive relationships is an obvious and essential key to success. In our schools, building positive relationships is, quite simply, job number one. Every educator in the school must realize that this core competency affects every aspect of school performance. Creating the types of relationships necessary for success requires the components of emotional intelligence examined by Goleman, Boyatzis, and McKee (2002), who identified four domains of emotional intelligence, including what they call "relationship management" with the specific components including: inspirational leadership, influence, developing others, change catalyst, conflict management, building bonds, teamwork and collaboration. They recognize the power of strong relationships in all organizations. "Positive groups help people make positive changes, particularly if the relationships are filled with candor, trust, and psychological safety" (p.163). Whether we are examining the principal-teacher relationship, the teacher-student relationship, or the school-community relationship, we must strive for associations built on the essential characteristics of honesty and openness in a safe and trusting environment.

Leadership experts Kouzes and Posner (1998) also establish a framework of essentials for cultivating and maintaining positive relationships, suggesting that caring about those with whom we work is essential to our effectiveness. Their seven essentials include: (1) setting clear standards, (2) expecting the best, (3) paying attention, (4) personalizing recognition, (5) telling the story, (6) celebrating together, and (7) setting the example. These seven characteristics of positive relationship building are central to the best practices carried out by teachers and school leaders who strive to make a difference in student and school performance. Marzano, Waters, and McNulty (2005) also stress this importance, identifying "relationships" as one of the twenty-one responsibilities school leaders must fulfill in order to positively impact student academic achievement. The authors suggest that educators within the school setting remain informed about significant personal situations facing staff members, acknowledging significant events in each other's lives and being aware of individual needs. It is impossible to separate the personal relationships we build with each other in our schools from the professional relationships we maintain. Educators committed to this core value recognize that the two go hand in hand and strive to create positive and personalized professional relationships as a result.

A key to building quality positive relationships within our schools is to establish trust among all stakeholders. This book is intended primarily for teacher leaders and school administrators. Establishing and maintaining trust between these two groups of educators is absolutely critical to school success. This relationship impacts every other relationship in the school community, most importantly, the teacher-student relationship. Schools at which administrators and teachers exhibit trusting, positive, and collaborative relationships exude a positive school culture that is palpable. In schools where trust is evident, with all educators joining together in pursuit of a common vision for the school and its students, learning soars (Gordon, 2001). Bryk and Schneider (2003) also examine the importance of trusting relationships, finding that schools with a high degree of relational trust are more likely to raise student achievement as compared to schools with lower degrees of relational trust. They offer four vital signs of such trust: (1) Respect, (2) Personal Regard, (3) Competence in Core Role Responsibilities, and (4)

Personal Integrity. Educators who treat all stakeholders and their ideas with dignity, who care about each other personally, who believe in one another's abilities, and who keep their word while putting the needs of children first are proficient in these four areas necessary to building trusting relationships.

The vast majority of educators enter the teaching profession predisposed to behaving along these lines and acting accordingly, once in place as teachers. Yet, over the course of a long, challenging, and stressful school year, even the best of us becomes too impatient or too busy or too overextended to remember the importance of these personal characteristics. As Todd has said repeatedly, our consistent adherence to these relational values cannot be overstated. We must adhere to them ten days out of ten (Whitaker, 2004). Even if we achieve 90% in this area, some within our school community will tend to remember the one day when we did not model these beliefs through our actions. Here again, even our superstar educators sometimes miss the 100% mark in this vitally-important area. The good news is, however, that just as we encourage teachers to allow students a chance to raise a failing grade or make up a grade of zero, we, too, can recover from a mistake should we happen to miss one day out of ten. The way we do so is simple and powerful, yet in our experience practiced only sporadically: we seek out the person whom we may have offended and offer a genuine apology. In schools, as in every other area of life, sincere apologies tend to repair damaged relationships.

Our schools are communities of human beings, and we are bound together by an ever-changing network of relationships as our student and teacher population changes from year to year. The skills that educators possess and practice that help build trusting relationships among these individuals will determine—to a great extent—the school's success. What follows are just a few ways we have found in which teachers and school leaders can employ specific relational strategies to improve student and school performance. As with the core factors of communication and observation, we cannot leave our commitment to building strong relationships to mere chance. Instead, we must monitor our actions in this area and intentionally plan for building and maintaining positive, personalized, professional relationships at our schools. The strategies outlined below require very little of the practitioners, other than a commitment to move from knowing they are important to actually following through and implementing them at their schools. Each suggestion below is rather simple to understand and enact and can be used at the elementary, middle, or high school level. In addition, we offer ideas for teachers and administrators, as well as ideas that pertain to both groups of educators.

Happy Holidays

In schools, particularly at the elementary level, holidays are a very important part of each school year. Kids at all levels still seem to look forward to each major holiday as it approaches, and teachers are often able to capitalize on this interest, designing curriculum activities related to holidays, ranging from Thanksgiving to Martin Luther King, Jr. Day. Holidays are also a time to pause and reflect on the relationships educators at schools have with each other. One practice we have used which strengthens relationships among the adults in our schools during the winter holiday season is sending a greeting card to the parent (or another close relative) of each teacher at our school. Throughout the semester, we take photos of each teacher (including custodians, cafeteria workers, administrators, and office staff) working with children and affix this photograph to a greeting card. Inside, we have printed a simple phrase stating, "We'd like to share one of our valued treasures at our school. She (He) makes our school a better place in which to learn. Happy Holidays!" We send these out just before leaving for our holiday break. The first year Todd did this, almost every teacher made it a point to let him know how much this meant to them and their families. Jeff also did this on an annual basis at a middle school where he served as principal. An added bonus is that each January we inevitably received many notes in return from our teachers' parents and family members, thanking us for taking the time to recognize their son or daughter in this way. In most schools, the winter break not only coincides with an important holiday, it also stands as the midpoint of another hectic school year. This is an ideal time to let every adult within the school know how important they are and to remind each other of our true purpose for serving as educators.

Cheers for Peers

Faculty meetings are a prime opportunity for building and maintaining relationships among all staff, often by celebrating the many accomplishments we have realized. One effective way to begin each faculty meeting, which takes only about five minutes, is something we refer to as "Cheers for Peers." This not only strengthens relationships among all teachers on staff, it also starts the faculty meeting off on a positive note. To begin such a practice, the principal or any teacher at the school places a dollar in a container for any teacher he or she wants to publicly recognize for any reason. This continues for several minutes, with any teacher wanting to recognize a colleague volunteering to add a dollar to the kitty for every person they wish to recognize. Whichever staff member recognizes the final colleague of the meeting keeps the container and brings it to the next faculty meeting to start the process again. The money raised through this simple act of affirmation can go to a school's sunshine fund or to a local charity. Oftentimes, we will have teachers contribute five or ten dollars and recognize an entire team of teachers. Cheers for Peers is a simple, quick, and fun way to strengthen relationships among the school staff.

More Faculty Meeting Celebrations

Faculty meetings should be meaningful events or should not occur at all. In many schools, whole faculty meetings are becoming less common, giving way, instead, to team, department, or professional learning community meetings. Whenever schools have the opportunity to gather as an entire faculty, however, school leaders should make certain that this time together is well spent. Any information that can be communicated in any way other than a face-to-face whole faculty setting should be thusly communicated, reserving these critically important meeting times for learning and celebration. Although successful school leaders may have several purposes for convening a whole faculty meeting, the ultimate goal should simply be for each teacher to leave the meeting more excited about teaching than they were when they arrived. Starting each meeting with a five minute "Cheers for Peers" activity is a good way to set the tone for accomplishing our goal. Closing each faculty meeting with recognitions is another way to have teachers leave faculty meetings more energized. We have worked with schools that have adopted the *FISH!* Philosophy (Lundin, Paul, & Christensen, 2000) and awarded "starfish" awards at the end of each faculty meeting. At these schools, teachers take turns acknowledging colleagues for something special they have done or achieved recently, presenting them with a starfish certificate and a small gift, provided by the school's administrators. Other schools have implemented a "This Bud's for You!" award at the close of each faculty meeting, whereby the principal provides a dozen roses and asks for 12 teachers to recognize a colleague for doing something good, presenting them with a rose for their good deed. At other schools, school leaders place the names of all teachers with perfect attendance for the month into a hat and draw out several names, presenting each with a gift certificate to a local restaurant to emphasize the importance of "being there" every day for students. While this is a fun and random way to offer a few nice gifts to teachers, it actually affirms one of our most important beliefs: teachers at our school make a huge difference in the lives of our students. Our students learn more when teachers are present each day. Both learning and behavior suffer when our regular teachers are absent. Not surprisingly, our very best teachers have exemplary attendance each and every year. They expect their students to attend school every day and model this behavior themselves. Awarding regular gift certificates for perfect teacher attendance is a small way of acknowledging our teachers who know that their presence makes a difference. Doing this during faculty meetings reinforces the fact that teacher attendance is a core value and helps to promote positive relationships with our superstar teachers.

Service Learning Opportunities

An extremely effective way to strengthen relationships among and between students, teachers, and administrators is through service learning opportunities. School accountability and standardized testing have tempted many schools to focus on improving test scores to the exclusion of equally important— and more meaningful and relevant—learning opportunities directly related to the world around them. Although we recognize the value of holding teachers, administrators, schools, and school districts accountable for raising test scores, we also recognize the need for kids to become actively and authentically engaged in real life learning opportunities. One way to do this while also forging strong and positive relationships among students and staff at a school are through service learning projects.

Opportunities for planning and implementing service learning projects abound in every school community in our nation. In order to successfully implement such events, start small and get students involved in deciding what type of project to embark upon. If students come up with their own idea for the service learning project to be implemented, they will be much more likely to follow through on it, learning more as a result and building relationships along the way. The possibilities for service learning ideas are unlimited and can be undertaken as an entire school project, an individual class or homeroom project, or grade-level project. We have seen such projects enacted once each school year or once each semester. At one school, a teacher of students who had been identified as at risk of dropping out decided to ask these students to consider and undertake such a project. One student in the group wanted to do something for the local fire department whose members had worked to save the life of her brother after a serious automobile accident. The class spent several weeks planning a Thanksgiving feast for the members of this fire department, preparing and delivering the food to the station on the final day of school before Thanksgiving break. While there, the fire department employees offered the students and teacher a tour of the facility and talked to them about the various aspects of their job. The local newspaper covered the event and published a nice article complete with photos of the students and the fire department personnel. The students learned a great deal of valuable life lessons throughout the project. At the same time, they bonded with each other, their teacher, and the members of the fire department whom they were serving.

Another teacher of gifted students at the same school enlisted the support of her students in a service learning project to help first graders attending a school in another part of the state with very limited resources. She asked each student in her class to purchase a copy of their favorite children's book, reading it and recording it on audiotape. She affixed a photo of each student inside the front cover of each book, placing individual books and tapes into plastic bags before shipping them to the school they wanted to help. As a result of this project, the first grade students who received the books learned more about reading, the middle school students who gave the books learned more about giving, and all students and teachers involved in the project learned about building positive relationships with others.

When Todd was principal at a junior high school, the students decided to plan a Christmas carnival for a preschool they chose to adopt. This school served students with various learning and physical handicaps. The event was a huge success, raising money to buy needed items for the younger children and providing a great deal of fun for both groups of children. In addition to communicating important messages to students about caring for others, the holiday carnival carried with it an added benefit: students were better behaved the rest of the week, teachers were in better spirits the rest of the week, and the school never had a problem with students teasing any of their physically or intellectually disabled peers after helping these younger disabled students.

One teacher who has successfully incorporated service learning opportunities into the curriculum suggested that the benefits are extraordinary. The thing about service learning that makes it so powerful is that because you change your role in the classroom, you change your relationship with the kids. Once you build strong relationships with kids, the power you have to reach them is incredible. Service learning projects are a valuable opportunity to reinforce our core curriculum goals while at the same time building powerful relationships among all involved.

Powerful Praise

In our schools, we are firm believers that students and teachers can never have "too much nice" (Whitaker, 2004, p. 51). One of our most important tasks as educators is to serve as models for our students, particularly by treating all school stakeholders with dignity and respect each and every day. As teachers and leaders, we must also not shirk our responsibility of holding students and each other accountable for doing our work and doing it well. We cannot be afraid to confront under-performance or inappropriate behaviors swiftly and firmly. Yet, we must not focus on all that is wrong, mistakes we make, and unpleasant obstacles that confront us. We suggested earlier that educators often find whatever it is they are looking for. While we cannot *overlook* things at our schools that are detrimental to learning or impediments to advancing our mission, we should focus on the good—which is abundant in every school at which we have worked throughout our careers. Finding people in our schools doing things right and praising them effectively for their performance increases the likelihood that they will con-tinue to do things right and that others will follow suit.

For some educators, praise can be a difficult issue. At times, we are afraid that we might overlook someone who wonders why they have not been recognized. Other educators say they are simply too busy to praise those in their classroom or school who are doing well. Still others fear that we might embarrass those we praise. Despite these arguments, we suggest that, done correctly, there is no such thing as too much praise. We follow five guidelines when praising students and teachers so that the praise has a positive effect. Such recognition must be (1) authen-tic, (2) specific, (3) immediate, (4) clean, and (5) private (Bissell, 1992). These guidelines apply when teachers praise students, when administrators praise teachers, when teachers praise administrators, and when teachers praise each other. They apply to the ideas we have suggested previously such as positive discipline referrals for students and Cheers for Peers at faculty meetings.

Most importantly, praise must be authentic. We simply must recognize our people for something genuine and true. To issue false praise is only counterproductive. To help ensure that the praise is authentic, it helps to be specific. Rather than stating that Joey did a nice job or that Mrs. Jones taught a nice lesson, we must hone in on precise behaviors they displayed that made their work exemplary. In addition, the more immediately we can provide praise, the more effective it is in reinforcing the behavior. Suggesting that praise must be "clean" implies that we must resist the temptation to add the word "but" after offering a compliment. It is OK—indeed, necessary—to point out those areas in which a teacher or student still needs to improve, but this must be separated from any authentic praise we are offering. Constructive criticism and genuine praise are ways that educators provide feedback so that others can improve. We must be careful not to destroy the value of praising by coupling it with an immediate criticism. Finally, it is often necessary to praise in private so that we do not embarrass the student, teacher, or administrator we are praising. There are times, of course, when we know it is right to recognize a student or colleague in front of a group or even the entire school. At other times, we must recognize that praising in public can be counterproductive to our goal of encouraging similar behaviors in that certain people tend to shy away from receiving public praise.

Successful schools are staffed with educators who make it their mission to create positive classroom cultures and a positive school culture. Praising those within the school who do right by students and each other is always the right thing to do. Some might say that in this era of increased school accountability, we are simply too busy to bother with frivolous old-fashioned ideas like praising students and teachers for their good deeds. In our opinion, the reverse is true. In order to hold students, teachers, administrators, and schools accountable for doing good work, it is more important than ever before to praise those who are achieving the specific results we are seeking.

A Personal Touch

Building positive relationships among all adults working within the school is the foundation for all that we do as educators and sets a good example for our students who see us interacting in a positive, personalized, and professional manner. In order to recognize important personal events in the lives of our colleagues, we must first demonstrate an awareness of each other's needs, interests, and special circumstances. We must show them that we care about them as individual human beings, not just as employees or co-workers. As educators, we are all in the "people" business. Educators model this focus on people by demonstrating an interest in the personal lives of their colleagues.

An important personal, as well as professional, accomplishment for educators is gaining some new level of education themselves. Not only is this typically a proud personal accomplishment, it again models that we practice what we preach to our students, which is that learning is a lifelong process and we must always strive to learn more. As a result, school leaders should make a conscious effort to recognize and celebrate any educational advancement faculty and staff members attain. The most frequent recognitions we made in this area while serving as principals included honoring teachers who had completed an advanced degree. Nearly every semester, we had at least one teacher or administrator who received a Master's, Specialist's, or Doctoral degree. We also recognized our paraprofessional workers who went back to school to obtain their Bachelor's degree or complete additional coursework and pass tests to become highly certified paraprofessional educators. In addition, we often worked with teachers who enrolled in a series of courses to obtain certification endorsements such as ESOL, Gifted, or Reading. We even recognized custodians and cafeteria workers who took courses to update their knowledge in important areas related to their field of expertise, facilities and school nutrition. Another accomplishment we always recognized publicly, which is both a personal and professional achievement, was publishing an article of some sort or presenting at a conference. The above examples of personal and professional growth are important opportunities for celebration. Successful schools recognize that such accomplishments are at the heart of our core business—learning—and make conscious efforts to recognize these at faculty meetings, in newsletters, and in personal notes or remarks.

We also recommend recognizing important personal events in the lives of Teachers, such as birthdays, weddings, births, and, unfortunately, deaths and illnesses that occur each year. As part of the "Thank God, It's Monday" memo explained in Chapter Two, principals can send out an email communication to the staff that includes the name of any staff member who is celebrating a birthday or other important occasion that week. Small gifts and a personal card given to each teacher on their birthday can also make a positive difference in building relationships. Staff members who get married or welcome a new baby into their family should also be celebrated. Schools with positive cultures that value personalized professional relationships typically hold after-school parties to honor these important personal events. We must be even more focused on being there for teachers who experience the loss of a family member or any other personal tragedy. Although nothing we do can erase the pain our teachers feel during these times, educators should make every effort to attend funeral services, visit staff members who are in the hospital, send notes of sympathy or concern, and provide meals, money, or any other support they can offer to suffering colleagues. In such situations, each individual teacher has unique needs and methods of coping, and we should strive to honor this, treating each situation differently, depending on the desires of the family. We have worked in schools that have established scholarship funds, purchased a wheelchair, organized a fun run/walk, and delivered weekly meals to staff members who were in need of support.

Schools that make a positive difference in the lives of the students they teach are typically staffed with teachers who make positive differences in each other's lives by establishing close personal, as well as professional, relationships. As educators, we are in the caring business. We must cultivate a culture of care within our schools, making it cool to care not only about our students, but about each other.

Word Power

The words we use at schools each day with our students and each other can have a powerfully positive—or negative—impact on those with whom we are working. It may seem like a small thing, but employed consistently over the course of a school year, using words of courtesy when interacting with others in the school helps to build positive relationships, enhancing the likelihood that student and teacher performance will improve. The words we choose to employ when asking or directing others to accomplish a task, encouraging others to adopt a change initiative, or discussing the school and its vision can impact the way others perceive us and our school. Words are powerful things and educators must select their words with purposeful care when dealing with parents, students, community members, and each other.

As an example, a small but powerful way to build better relationships through our diction includes incorporating the following simple words as often as humanly possible when interacting with school stakeholders: (1) please, (2) thank you, (3) we, (4) our, and (5) I'm sorry. At successful schools staffed with educators dedicated to making a positive difference, teachers and administrators use these words regularly and sincerely. Saying "Please" and "Thank you" requires absolutely no effort and—spoken consistently and sincerely over time—is almost certain to pay regular dividends. Great educators realize that using these words of courtesy requires no extra effort and helps strengthen relationships; therefore, they never ask a custodian, secretary, or one another to do anything without using the words "please" and "thank you." Whether this is a face-to-face communication or a written communication, great educators are vigilant about including these words to accompany any request they make or direction they give. As important as it is to use these words when interacting with adults at the school, it is equally important to use these with the students we teach. Including "please" and "thank you" when conversing with students not only increases the chances that they will work harder to please us, it also serves as a powerful model for how they should treat others. Opportunities for incorporating these simple, but powerful, words into our everyday use abound. In the classroom setting, moving from, "Johnny, stop talking" to "Johnny, please stop talking; thank you" is a simple way of increasing the likelihood that Johnny will comply with our directive. Each day, there are literally hundreds of opportunities for educators to create stronger relationships with students and each other simply by adding these words to the sentences they are already uttering. Say "please" a lot. Say "thank you" a lot. People with whom you interact will notice and appreciate this and will be more likely to respond in kind. Treating others with simple dignity and respect on a consistent basis is contagious and carries with it absolutely no downside.

Two other small, but monumentally important, words great educators incorporate into their daily lexicon in place of two other words are "we" and "our" as substitutes for "I and "my." We often meet principals who are in the habit of talking about "my school" or "my football coach" or suggesting that "I implemented a plan . . . " or "I made AYP again this year." In such instances, a subtle shift in pronoun usage to include the entire school community can send a powerful message that accomplishments achieved and decisions reached are the results of collective, rather than individual, efforts. By adopting such inclusive words, we are not only speaking more accurately ("my" school?), we are also modeling for everyone who hears us that our schools are collaborative, collegial communities in which all stakeholders are working toward reaching shared goals. Administrators and school leaders who move from, "I am disappointed in the 8th grade math performance on the state tests" to "We need to examine our math results and see how we can work together to improve our performance" are less likely to create a sense that blame is being assigned and more likely to create a feeling that, together, improved performance will be attained.

For some reason, many educators with whom we have worked have a difficult time adding what we consider perhaps the two most powerful words of all when interacting with others, especially students and parents: "I'm sorry." Todd has written and spoken extensively about the effectiveness of this powerful phrase, particularly when dealing with a parent who is upset about something that happened at school. No matter what the specific situation is, whenever any parent, student, or teacher is upset about something that happened at school, great educators who first respond with, "I'm sorry that happened" have taken a dramatic step toward defusing the situation and creating a better relationship with the person who is upset. By stating that we are sorry something has happened, we are not agreeing that we erred nor are we accepting blame for the situation. We are simply sorry that something has happened that resulted in making one of our students, teachers, or parents upset. At times, we may take steps to rectify the situation if indeed a wrong has been committed. At other times, we simply listen and reiterate the fact that we are sorry something has happened. Although these situations typically arise when dealing with difficult parents, it is just as important to let our students know we are sorry when something goes wrong in their lives or if we have treated them unfairly. Most human beings are forgiving by nature. Saying "I'm sorry" when we have made a mistake and genuinely want to atone for it often resolves the situation and repairs the relationship with the offended party. Saying, "I am sorry that happened" even when we have done no wrong, but are speaking with an upset person, also helps to soothe situations that threaten to damage relationships at our schools.

When posting job vacancies, nearly all organizations—including school systems—list "effective oral and written communication skills" as a core requirement necessary for success, yet we often overlook the power of our daily language as we interact with students, parents, and colleagues at our schools. Incorporating simple words of dignity and respect as a matter of practice can have a dramatic and positive impact on the relationships that exist among all school stakeholders.

Repairing Relationships

Another aspect of relationships we must consider is repairing ones that are damaged for one reason or another. Building and maintaining positive relationships is perhaps the single most important charge of leaders within any organization. Without strong relationships between people working together for a common cause, the organization is not likely to achieve optimal levels of success. Therefore, we begin with the premise that educators in great schools work ten days out of ten to treat every member of the school community with dignity and respect. Even if we achieve 90% success in this key area, others are likely to remember the 10% of the time that we failed more readily than the many times we acted properly. Once damaged, a relationship may never be the same again. At the same time, we live in a world in which even the best of us make mistakes in our treatment of each other and there are inevitable occasions during the course of a long school year when relationships are, indeed, damaged. While we work hard to prevent this, at times it does happen. When it does, great educators work even harder to resolve the conflict and restore the positive relationship. When relationships between teachers and parents, teachers and students, principals and teachers, or one teacher and another teacher go awry for any reason, great educators do whatever it takes to repair the relationship.

As we suggested previously, one way great educators repair relationships is by saying "I'm sorry that happened" when someone with whom we interact is upset about anything. A more proactive approach to repairing relationships, however, is doing little things as a matter of routine, which helps to repair relationships *before* they are even damaged. Great teachers do this when they start off one class lesson by apologizing for not explaining some concept carefully enough the day before. This may or may not have been the case, but great teachers want students to know that they hold themselves to high standards and are upset with themselves if they feel that they did not put forth their very best performance. Great principals do this when they apologize to teachers at a faculty meeting for not being as visible recently in their classrooms as they would like. Again, teachers may be thinking that this principal is a regular visitor to their classroom, but great principals know they can never be visible enough to students and teachers and apologize when they feel they are not there as often as they would like. Great teachers and great administrators proactively repair relationships by calling parents of kids who frequently misbehave and letting them know that their child did something outstanding or had a good day. The more often educators practice what we call "repairing on the fly," the less often they will find themselves repairing a relationship after the damage has already occurred, which takes a great deal more effort and is decidedly less effective than heading off potential problems before they arise.

Great educators work hard to keep their relationships with students, parents, and each other in good repair. On those rare occasions when great educators find that a relationship is damaged, they work immediately and decisively to repair the relationship, oftentimes simply by listening actively and starting the healing process by saying, "I'm sorry this happened." Why is it that great teachers seem to do this naturally and our mediocre teachers have such a difficult time doing this? We have found that in many instances, mediocre educators lack the self-confidence to engage in repairing activities—in particular, the ability to apologize. The number one gift that exemplary teachers and administrators can give to their colleagues—and their students—is confidence. Educators who are confident in their abilities do not let pride or ego get in the way of achieving success in their core business: student learning. Such educators are constantly—and consciously—working to repair relationships, both proactively and in response to situations in which a relationship has been damaged in some way.

Clarifying the C.O.R.E.: Relationships

As we stated at the outset of this book, the four dimensions of teaching, learning, and leading, which we both value above all others and which pervade all areas of the school, ultimately impacting its climate, culture, teacher morale, and student academic achievement, are *Communication, Observation, Relationships,* and *Expectations.* Educators committed to making a difference in the lives of students, each other, and the school itself must plan for excelling in each of these core areas. Although most would agree that consciously cultivating, building, and maintaining positive professional and personal relationships within a school contribute to its overall success, it is not always the case that specific practices exist for ensuring that continuous relationship-building occurs. Educators who want to positively impact the schools in which they serve must strategically and purposefully engage in activities that allow them to forge and maintain collegial and collaborative relationships among and between students, teachers, administrators, and parents.

Our purpose in the previous section of this chapter has simply been to offer a few simple, but specific, strategies that educators can employ to effectively and consistently build positive, personalized, professional relationships within the school community. Additional opportunities for doing so are virtually infinite in scope and size. In schools today, nearly all educators would agree that the quality of the relationships within the school determine, in large part, how successful that school will be in terms of student and teacher performance. Strong relationships are built on a number of characteristics, but the foremost one in our experience is that of trust. In closing this chapter on the importance of relationships within schools, we wish to examine the issue of trust. High levels of trust result in healthy, positive relationships; conversely, in schools with little trust, relationships—and, ultimately, student learning—suffer. In our experience, perhaps no characteristic is more important to building successful relationships and productive teams than that of trust. Establishing trusting relationships among all stakeholders, however, is not easy and schools with high levels of trust among all stakeholders appear to be the exception rather than the rule. Yet, this vital quality is of such import that it must become and remain a foremost value and focus of any educator striving to positively impact schools. Sebring and Bryk (2000) report that in schools that are improving, levels of trust and cooperation among adults are high, with students reporting that teachers care about them and that they experience greater academic challenges. In contrast, schools that are experiencing declining or flat scores are staffed by teachers who are more likely to state that they do not trust one another. With trust playing such an important role in building the relationships that are critical to school success, it is important to examine what, exactly, constitutes trust.

There are many components of trusting relationships. Tschannen-Moran and Hoy (1998) identified five key components to measure trustworthiness:

(1) Benevolence—those working together have each other's best interest at heart and will protect those interests.
(2) Reliability—those working together can depend upon each other to come through.
(3) Competence—those working together believe in one another's ability to perform the tasks required by their positions.
(4) Honesty—those working together can be counted on to represent situations fairly and with integrity.
(5) Openness—those working together freely share information with one another.

Schools that are staffed with educators who are benevolent, reliable, competent, honest, and open are more likely to establish positive working relationships characterized by high levels of trust, resulting in increased productivity and performance. More recently, Lencioni (2005) has worked with hundreds of teams within a variety of organizations in establishing trust among team members. Through his work, he has identified four key points related to building trust:

(1) Trust is the foundation of teamwork.
(2) On a team, trust is all about vulnerability, which is difficult for most people.
(3) Building trust takes time, but the process can be greatly accelerated.
(4) Like a good marriage, trust on a team is never complete; it must be maintained over time.

Each point above, of course, is interrelated. For example, while it is true that vulnerability can be difficult to accept, we can accelerate this component of trust by encouraging risk and experimentation without fear of reprisal should efforts fail. Lencioni's belief that building positive relationships with others is the foundation for teamwork holds powerful connotations for educators, nearly all of whom find themselves working as members of a variety of teams. In order to effectively fulfill any leadership responsibility on these teams, we must first demonstrate an awareness of each other's needs, interests, and special circumstances. We must show that we care about others as individual human beings, not just as co-workers, students, or parents. Realizing that ours is a people-oriented profession, great educators focus on people first and programs second.

A great many factors contribute to the state of relationships within a school, but we agree with Lencioni (2005) and Tschannen-Moran and Hoy (1998) that the foundation for strong relationships among teams and individuals within an organization is trust. While Lencioni highlights the importance of trust as a key to success in any organization, Bryk and Schneider (2002) specifically examined the relationship between trust and student achievement in schools, finding that there is a connection between the level of trust in a school and student learning. They found that in schools with high levels of trust among the adults working within, conditions were more conducive for initiating and sustaining the activities and changes necessary to affect school improvement. We are firm believers that forging strong relationships is a core foundation for successful schools and that building trust is a core foundation for establishing these strong relationships. Of course, building strong relationships by establishing trust is not as easy as it sounds. Many obstacles await us and we must consciously plan for success in this all-important area.

Common barriers to building and maintaining trust in schools are many. Frequent changes in school leadership, teacher turnover, teacher isolation, top-down decision making, ineffective communication, and a lack of follow-through are just a few obstacles educators face in creating and maintaining trusting, positive relationships in schools. Rather than focusing on these obstacles, however, great educators instead realize that the urgency and importance of building positive relationships compels them to act in ways that break down these barriers to success. In the previous section of this chapter, we offered just a few specific strategies that we have either used ourselves or that we have seen other educators use to achieve success in fulfilling the responsibility of relationship building. Every principal and every teacher with whom we have worked has in their own "bag of tricks" a plentitude of additional ideas that are equally effective. In our experience, we have found that successful educators establish consistent methods for employing these strategies, relying not on random acts of kindness, but on a planned, coordinated, and comprehensive belief system designed to sustain strong relationships that carry schools through times of stress, celebration, challenges, and change.

The strategies we have in our bag of tricks are not nearly as important as the day-to-day behaviors we exhibit as we go about our business as educators. While every relationship within a school is important to its success, we have found that success begins with developing strong relationships between the principal and the teachers working together within a school. Typically, if this relationship is strong, an actual "trickle-down" effect results, which impacts the entire school. Teachers, in turn, have better relationships with students. As a result of this strong teacher-student bond, relationships between parents and educators are strengthened. Consider the list of ways to establish trusting and positive relationships below. First, consider it from the administrator-teacher perspective. We believe that these traits are vital to creating trust between teachers and administrators. Next, consider these traits from the teacher-student or the teacher-parent perspective. Once again, we find that these are the critical components to success. Here, then, is perhaps our "Top Ten Trust Traits" for behaving in a manner conducive to effective relationship-building among all school stakeholders. While all of us have our own favorite ideas—even gimmicks—for relationship building, these daily behaviors will supersede any one-time idea we can share, no matter how great.

(1) *Be There.*
(2) *Show You Care.*
(3) *Provide Resources.*
(4) *Communicate Regularly.*

(5) *Involve Others.*
(6) *Celebrate Success.*
(7) *Value Diversity and Dissent.*
(8) *Support Innovation.*
(9) *Address Underperformance.*
(10) *Demonstrate Personal Integrity.*

Take a look at these simple phrases again, from each of the perspectives listed above, examining how they apply to students, teachers, parents, and administrators. Educators committed to these behaviors on a daily basis are master relationship builders who cultivate a sense of trust among people with whom they interact. Moreover, success on the part of our stellar educators in these areas can have a contagious effect, impacting others within the building and the entire community, creating an atmosphere in which everyone plays a small part in something big: a school committed to a culture of caring.

Relationships are of vital importance in our lives as educators and one of our four core factors for impacting school success. Collectively, educators within the school must establish consistent strategies designed to strengthen relationships among all school stakeholders. More important than any single strategy, however, are the daily behaviors described above which, over time, ensure that trust exists within the school, resulting in the strong relationships critical to its success. Great educators clarify the core value of relationships at the outset of each year, with administrators and teachers working together to remind each other of important behaviors and practices in this area and addressing openly and honestly any concerns, setting a course for acting in strategic ways in order to embody this value throughout the school year to ensure the optimal performance of all with whom they work.

Chapter Five

Expectations: Strategies for Success

For several years early in our teaching careers, we also served as basketball coaches. One quote we often shared with athletes on our teams went something like this: "Whether you think you can or think you can't, you're right." Many times, our athletes performed at the level of their own—and their coaches'—expectations. Those teams that thought they could and would win often did, even when they were clearly out-manned in terms of physical stature and skills. Such teams seem to simply will themselves to victory, regardless of the challenges that face them. In our schools, we have experienced a similar phenomenon. Schools staffed with educators who expect students to succeed and who consistently and clearly communicate this expectation to students and parents, often do. Our expectations of our students, our schools, and one another influence how well each will perform.

Recently, one of us attended a high school orientation for a daughter who is entering high school in a few months. Each teacher and administrator who took to the podium to speak to the rising 9th graders and their parents seemed to communicate a consistent message: high school would be very difficult and very different from middle school. It appeared that even if our children were gifted students who had earned all A's throughout middle school, we should still be wary and prohibit them from enrolling in all honors and AP classes at the high school level. One teacher went so far as to share the following statistic with us: of the 500 students currently in the 9th grade at that school, only 18 had earned straight A's through the first semester. Although likely not the intended outcome, many students and parents left the orientation session that evening fearful of enrolling in the school's most rigorous courses offered. On the other hand, we have visited high schools of similar size and with similar demographics that seem to challenge and invite students to seek out the most rigorous class load appropriate, letting students and parents know the advantages of doing so and assuring them that teachers were in place who would do everything necessary to help interested students succeed at high levels.

In working with educators at all levels across the country, we continue to emphasize what is perhaps our foremost requirement for success: educators must clearly establish high expectations for students and then set about building relationships with them such that they will want to meet our expectations. Perhaps nothing influences how well our students perform in terms of academics and behavior as much as the expectations we have for them in these areas and the firm, fair, and consistent manner in which we monitor and adhere to them. As a result, all educators working within the school must consciously focus on establishing high expectations that are clear and attainable for all students. In addition, we must hold ourselves and our parents accountable, expecting each other to take actions that will ensure that students want to meet our expectations and are able to do so. Educators focused on and skilled in the area of setting expectations for learning recognize the multiple facets related to expectations and purposefully plan for fulfilling all components of this core responsibility outlined below in a systematic, consistent manner.

Facets of Expectations

The act or state of anticipating an outcome and determining the probability that it will occur. To set goals and guidelines for anticipated levels of performance.

Educators effective in the core skill of expectations:

♦ Anticipate	♦ Envision	♦ Look For	♦ Suppose
♦ Assume	♦ Exact	♦ Predict	♦ Surmise
♦ Believe	♦ Forecast	♦ Presume	♦ Suspect
♦ Calculate	♦ Foresee	♦ Rely Upon	♦ Think
♦ Call For	♦ Hope	♦ Require	♦ Trust
♦ Count On	♦ Imagine	♦ See Coming	♦ Want
♦ Demand	♦ Insist On	♦ Sense	♦ Watch For

Effective Expectations Defined

We are avid believers that the expectations educators hold for students, each other, and themselves impact student and school performance. In terms of teacher expectations, probably the most famous study in the area of how teacher expectations influenced student outcomes is Rosenthal and Jacobson's *Pygmalion in the Classroom* (1968), in which teachers were told at the outset that 20% of their students (randomly selected) were identified as "spurters," whose academic performance would likely grow dramatically during the year. Sure enough, at the end of the year, these 20% significantly outgained the 80% who were not identified as "spurters" on an academic achievement test. Marzano (2007) elaborates on how teachers influence student performance through expectations:

> A teacher's beliefs about students' chances of success in school influence the teacher's actions with students, which in turn influence students' achievement. If the teacher believes students can succeed, she tends to behave in ways that help them succeed. If the teacher believes that students cannot succeed, she unwillingly tends to behave in ways that subvert student success or at least do not facilitate student success. This is perhaps one of the most powerful hidden dynamics of teaching because it is typically an unconscious activity. (p. 162)

Just as teacher expectations influence student outcomes, we feel that administrator expectations influence teacher—and, in turn, student—outcomes. Together, teacher and administrator expectations can greatly impact school outcomes—for better or worse.

How can teachers and administrators behave in ways that communicate to students that we expect them to learn at high levels? Marzano (2007) discusses two categories of teacher behaviors that communicate expectations to students: (1) affective tone and (2) quality of interactions. Affective tone refers to the extent to which teachers establish positive feelings, emotions, and climates in the classroom. In terms of quality of interactions, research has shown that teachers differ in their interactions with high versus low expectancy students. To avoid differential treatment in terms of affective tone, Marzano suggests examining whether we treat low expectancy students differently by:

+ Making less eye contact
+ Smiling less
+ Making less physical contact or maintaining less proximity
+ Engaging in less playful or light dialogue.

Virtually no teacher we know would do any of the above consciously or with the intent of treating any student unfairly, yet we must take care to ensure that we are not unwittingly communicating to any student that we hold them in any less regard than our highest achieving students. Relative to quality of interactions, Marzano (2007) suggests examining whether we treat low-expectancy students differently by:

+ Calling on them less
+ Asking them less challenging questions
+ Not delving into their answers as deeply
+ Rewarding them for less rigorous responses.

Again, any teacher who exhibits the above traits most likely does not do so maliciously. In fact, the opposite is probably true, in that they think are doing low-expectancy students a favor by letting them off the hook. Again, it is important for all educators to expect all students to perform at high levels. Accepting anything less communicates a powerfully negative message.

Blackburn (2007) also addresses expectations and suggests there are three ways to incorporate high expectations into every classroom: (1) through teacher words, (2) through teacher actions, and (3) through teacher expectations of each individual working together. The language we use with students clearly reflects our beliefs. Students will follow our model when they hear us using excuses or saying we can't do something. Even more important, our actions must show that we expect all students to learn. By calling on all students and requiring all students to demonstrate their understanding of the content, we are communicating our expectations through our actions. Finally, we must cultivate a classroom culture whereby students expect *each other* to learn, participate, and behave properly. Through our modeling, students can begin to reinforce positive learning and behavioral actions for each other. Sadly, too many of our students have absolutely no vision of anything for themselves other than where they are right now. Teachers and administrators can help kids create a vision for themselves through their words (including affective tone) and actions (including quality of interactions). There is perhaps no greater gift we can give students than this.

A wealth of additional research supports the idea that expectations influence outcomes within schools. According to Edmonds (1986), schools that establish high expectations for all students and provide support necessary to achieve these expectations have high rates of success. Brook, Nomura, and Cohen (1989) found that high expectations and a school culture that values student participation mitigates risk factors in adolescents' use of alcohol and drugs. High expectations with concomitant support is a critical factor in decreasing the number of students who drop out while increasing the number of students who go on to college (Mehan, Hubbard, & Villanueva, 1994). Rutter, et al. (1979) found that high expectations on the part of educators in successful schools helped to develop student self-esteem and self-efficacy. In his 1983 review of teacher expectations research, Brophy estimated that 5 to 10 percent of the variance in student performance is attributable to differential treatment accorded them based on differences in their teachers' expectations of them. This estimate alone is enough to suggest that we must purposefully examine our expectations for students and our practices that relate to these expectations.

Teacher expectations can be self-fulfilling. The power of belief one person has in another can become a propelling force for that person to begin believing in himself. Although intellectual ability obviously affects student academic performance, we are convinced that hard work and effort are even more important in determining a student's level of performance. Most teachers would agree that their own success was a result of hard work and effort. As educators, we must continue to communicate this message to students, expecting them to achieve at high levels as a result of their work and effort, rather than any innate ability. Of course, it would be folly to suggest that simply having high expectations for students is all that is needed for them to succeed. We must offer more than platitudes in this area, using this *belief* as a launching pad for *actions* designed to communicate, reinforce, and model behaviors aimed at following through on our commitment that all students can and will learn at high levels. If educators are truly committed to creating schools in which expectations are high for all learners, it is imperative that we create learning environments in which teachers, students, parents, and administrators work together to communicate to all students three crucial messages: (1) The work we do is important, (2) You can do it, and (3) We will not give up on you (Howard, 1990; Saphier, 2005).

Induction

When does new teacher induction begin? Many educators assume that it begins—at best—on the first day of new teacher orientation before the students come back to school to start the new year. However, we believe that induction begins during the interview process. As soon as the interviewing team realizes that they are talking to a candidate with the potential to be hired, members should consciously begin asking questions in a way that sets the stage for future employment at the school as a teacher. For example, if the school is considering a plan whereby teachers would regularly observe each other teaching, an administrator or teacher leader on the interviewing team might well ask, "How would you feel about observing other teachers at our school and having them observe in your classroom?" Obviously, if the prospective teacher wants the job, he or she will likely respond that this is the greatest idea since the wheel, but our point is to ask questions that set the stage for our expectations in significant areas related to our school culture. It is important to let the teaching candidate know through purposeful questioning our expectations in terms of how we treat students and how we treat each other.

Once we have hired a new teacher to our school, the formal induction process begins in earnest, of course. One tool we have used successfully to communicate expectations as part of our induction process is what we call the "Progressive Dinner."

During the Progressive Dinner, we ask a team of returning teacher leaders to plan a two-hour induction program, which outlines many of our school expectations—for teachers, for students, for administrators, and for parents. Although there are a number of ways this can be organized, we have typically had a team of four or more teachers volunteer to host this event. New teachers move to four different classrooms, spending 30 minutes in each, learning about some aspect of the school and its expectations while at the same time enjoying a meal. In the first classroom, new teachers enjoy an appetizer of some sort while learning about, perhaps, our expectations for teacher collaboration. After a short break, they move to a classroom in a completely different part of the building, enjoying a salad and learning about our expectations for student behavior. Next, these new teachers will move to two final classrooms in different parts of the school enjoying their entrée in one and dessert and coffee in the final classroom while again learning about our expectations. This process allows for a great deal of interaction between new and returning teachers while sharing lunch in a fun way. In addition, we always ask the four returning teachers to have their classrooms fully organized and decorated so that our new teachers will observe four classrooms that are physically arranged into inviting learning environments, subtly communicating our expectations for creating classrooms that are exciting and appealing to our students.

There are limitless ways that schools can organize the content and flow of the new teacher progressive dinner. Regardless of how this is organized, it can be a fun and creative way to communicate expectations to a hugely important part of a school: its newest teachers.

No Pecking Order

Another message we communicate to new teachers as soon as possible is that we do not have a "pecking order" at our school in which veteran teachers "earn" certain rights and privileges due solely to their seniority within the school. This is another message we communicate at the very first interview, letting new teachers know that we desire and expect their input on every issue related to teaching and learning at our school. One question we typically ask during the interview to communicate this expectation goes something like this: "At our school, we do not want to hire teachers who become more like the other teachers at our school once we hire them. Instead, we want to hire teachers who are so outstanding that we want our school to become more like them in some way. What will you bring to our school that is so outstanding that all teachers at our school will want to emulate you in that area?" A question along these lines sends a powerful message that we expect new teachers to voice their opinions and share their expertise in order to make an immediate impact upon our school.

Rewarding excellence rather than mere seniority honors our very best teachers. Of course, many of our finest teachers are veteran teachers, so we often look to them to lead their colleagues in a variety of ways, including mentoring our new teachers. At the same time, we realize that every school at which we have worked seems to have one or more teachers on board who have worked in the same role for many years and believe that through longevity alone they have "earned" the right to teach only the "best" students or to not volunteer for any extracurricular responsibilities. Thankfully, this attitude of entitlement is less prevalent than it was several years ago as educators realize it not only dishonors our new teachers who are capable of contributing in a variety of ways and whose voices should be heard, it also affronts those veteran teachers who are still energized about their school and want to learn and work as much as possible on its behalf. Although it is important to support teachers who are new to the school in a variety of ways and through a formal and informal induction program, it is equally important that we send them a clear message that we expect them to learn quickly so that they can lead sooner rather than later. Letting them know that there is no pecking order as part of the school culture sends a powerful message of expectation that our best teachers—new and veteran alike—appreciate.

Three Crucial Messages

Although it is of paramount importance that we set, communicate, and adhere to explicit expectations for teachers, it is equally important that we do the same for our students. At the outset of each year, all educators must clearly communicate extremely specific and lofty expectations for student performance. It is important that this is done on the very first day of the school year. Done effectively, educators can then spend the remaining 179 days of the school year establishing relationships with students so that they will actually *want* to meet these expectations. A key to success in this area is that every educator in the building enforce those expectations established for students at the beginning of the year in a firm, fair, and consistent manner.

Expectations must be set at the school level and at the classroom level. All educators in the building must meet each year to establish school-wide expectations for student behavior as well as student work. School leaders cannot allow individual teachers to shirk their responsibility in enforcing these expectations. For example, if a school-wide expectation is that all students arrive to class on time, it is imperative that each teacher adhere to this expectation consistently. When all educators in the building hold identical expectations in areas such as this and adhere to them consistently, it is remarkable how well students act in accordance with them. At the same time, it is perfectly natural and acceptable for individual teachers to have classroom-specific expectations that may vary from room to room. As long as individual classroom expectations do not conflict with school-wide expectations and the school's mission, vision, and values, teachers should be encouraged to create, communicate, and enforce expectations for student academic and behavioral performance within their individual classrooms.

Although many of the expectations we establish for students relate to student behavior, it is also vitally important that we establish expectations for student work. For doing so, we again find no clearer message to communicate our expectations in this area than the three crucial messages described previously: (1) The work assigned is extremely important; (2) You can do it; and (3) We will not give up on you (Howard, 1990; Saphier, 2005). A non-negotiable component of any successful school culture should include a focus on student work. Each of the three statements above must first be examined closely. If we believe that all work assigned is extremely important, we must avoid assigning "busy" work or homework simply for the sake of assigning it. Every assignment we expect students to complete should be absolutely essential to their mastering a skill or concept related to the curriculum. We must also communicate through our words and actions that the work we are assigning is something that each student is capable of successfully completing. By now, we all know that not all children learn at the same rate and in the same way, but if they are in our schools we must give them the gift of confidence in their ability to learn and perform the required work.

Finally, we know that many of our students will struggle at some point in their academic career. Again, we must communicate that this is OK and that we are there to help them. One way we can do this is through school-wide interventions, such as carving out extra time for academic assistance for students who need additional support. Another way we do this is by communicating with our students and their parents through formative assessments, letting them know where the student currently is, where they need to go next, and how—together—we can get there. High-performing schools also succeed in this area by creating school cultures that hold students accountable for completing all assignments through initiatives such as the one described below.

ZAP

Nearly every teacher we know, beginning in Kindergarten and moving all the way through 12th grade, struggles to a certain extent in getting every student to complete every assignment. In every school we have visited, the issue of "zeroes" presents itself as a controversial topic and—more importantly— an obstacle to student success. Since there are students at every school in our country who at times do not turn in an assignment, this is not a variable among schools. Instead, the variable is how we, as educators, respond when students do not turn in work. The expectation that educators within a school have regarding zeroes will determine, to a large extent, how many zeroes are assigned. Stated simply, we believe that the appropriate consequence for a student who does not complete an assignment is to insist that he completes the assignment. Whether the assignment is completed at home, during a working lunch period, during a detention, or during a Saturday school session is up to those working within individual schools. However, it is absolutely necessary that every educator in the entire school expect and insist that every child complete every assignment.

At several schools we have visited that have succeeded in establishing a "no zero" policy, teachers, administrators, and parents have worked together to adopt a **ZAP** Policy: **Z**eroes **A**ren't **P**ermitted. Although such programs vary from school to school, we have seen it work successfully when teachers take turns hosting a before or after school "ZAP" session, at which students who have failed to turn in an assignment in any class attend and complete the missed assignment. Typically, if each teacher at the school volunteers to supervise just a few ZAP sessions, the school can hold such a makeup opportunity for students one or more days each week of the school year. Knowing that zeroes are a primary reason children fail classes at all grade levels, parents are typically supportive of such programs and ensure that their children attend these before- or after-school sessions.

Of course, if we are to expect every child to complete every piece of work assigned, we must also examine our own practices in the area of assigning classwork and homework. Parents and students should expect us to assign only meaningful work that is necessary in order for students to master core concepts. Getting every student to complete and turn in every assignment is not necessarily easy, but it is, to coin a phrase from Michael Fullan (2003), one of our moral imperatives as educators. Rarely is anything worth doing in our schools easy, but if every teacher and administrator adheres consistently to the expectation that every assignment will be a meaningful one and must be completed, over time the idea that all student work must be turned in becomes engrained into the school's culture. As students begin to realize that they are going to have to do the work either sooner or later, they eventually realize that they might as well turn it in sooner.

Assigning zeroes is an easy way out—for both the teacher and the student. We have found that zeroes are ineffective in achieving the desired outcome in that they simply are not motivating to the students who typically receive them. On the other hand, many of our valedictorians and other high-performing students *would* be motivated by a zero. Not surprisingly, though, these students typically do not receive such grades. Therefore, the best thing we can do as educators to motivate our students to complete every assignment is simply to establish and enforce a school-wide set of expectations that all assigned work will be completed and all students will be held accountable for completing every missed assignment rather than settling for a zero. Expecting and insisting that "Zeroes Aren't Permitted" is a critically important way in which successful schools impact student learning.

Pay It Forward

Previously, we mentioned that one of Todd's goals as principal was to create a school culture in which it was "cool to care." Jeff, as principal, emphasized as part of the school culture an atmosphere in which every student and adult focused on three overarching actions each day as they went about their day: working hard, having fun, and being nice to every person they met. With all the demands facing schools today, it has become increasingly necessary for educators to possess a wealth of technical knowledge, expertise, and skills to best address the needs of all learners. Yet, for all its importance, the *science* of teaching is worthless if we are not also adept at the *art* of teaching. Creating school cultures in which students and teachers alike care about each other, work hard each day, have fun each day, and are nice to each other on a daily basis is certainly not rocket science, yet it is very difficult to achieve on a consistent and pervasive basis and is every bit as important as writing detailed lesson plans or creating formal intervention plans.

For years we have observed firsthand that working hard and having fun seem to go hand in hand at schools. Those teachers who have the most fun are also the ones who work the hardest. In addition to their teaching duties, they typically sponsor or attend after-school events, reveling in the chance to see their own students or perhaps those they do not teach participate in drama, sports, chorus, or club activities. Students note when their teachers are present at these events and tend to work harder and behave better for teachers who support them and their school in this way. We have also observed that students within the classroom setting tend to work harder in those classrooms in which fun and learning seem to be intertwined. Our very best teachers manage to make learning fun through creative, hands-on lessons and an enthusiastic, humorous teaching style. In such fun and lively classrooms, students actually work harder than in classrooms that are routinely marked by silent and individual seatwork. Although working hard and having fun should be at the center of all that we do in schools, we must also never underestimate the importance of being nice to one another and caring about all within our schools and our school community. One way we have seen schools achieve success in this aspect of school culture is by establishing an informal "Pay It Forward" expectation among all students and adults at the school.

Based on the popular movie of the same name, the idea of Pay It Forward is simply to ask—and expect—that no good deed go for naught. Instead, school leaders ask that any student or adult at the school who is the recipient of a kind act, gesture, or gift respond not by returning the favor to the giver, but by paying it forward to a third party in some way. A teacher who receives a nice note from the principal might, in turn, write a positive discipline referral on one of her students. A 6th grade student who receives assistance from an 8th grade student mentor might seek out another student in his class to help or might even reach out to help a 5th grader at the elementary school. The possibilities for such a program are endless and require little in the way of formal procedures or paperwork. Typically, all it takes is for teachers and administrators to publicize this practice as part of the school's value system and remind students and each other about it regularly through announcements, newsletters, and by periodically recognizing students and teachers who have gone above and beyond in this area by practicing especially meaningful acts of kindness.

We have also seen something similar occur at schools during the holiday season, as students and teachers embarked upon a "Random Acts of Christmas" initiative. At one school, each student and teacher was given a small card explaining the program. Each person at the school was to do something nice for another in an anonymous manner, finding a way to leave the card with the recipient so that they could pass it on again if they chose. For the entire month, nice things happened, as teachers secretly paid for each other's lunch in the cafeteria or students cleaned a teacher's classroom after school for a teacher. Admittedly, ideas such as Pay It Forward and Random Acts of Christmas have little direct bearing on whether a school makes AYP or a student exceeds expectations on standardized tests. Yet, expecting all students and teachers in the school to treat one another with kindness and caring models much more important life lessons and—indirectly, we suspect—results in increased student and teacher performance, to boot.

Collaboration

By now, almost every school that we visit emphasizes to a certain extent the concept of professional collaboration in order to improve teaching practices and—ultimately—student results. Although almost every such school proclaims itself a "professional learning community" (PLC) we have found that very few actually bear much resemblance to the concept of PLCs first described by DuFour and Eaker (1998). Those schools that truly are upholding the tenets of PLCs with a focus on collaboration, a focus on learning, and a focus on results are almost certain to have reaped huge benefits in terms of both student and teacher performance. The difference between schools that say they are

PLCs and schools that actually behave as PLCs is largely attributable to the expectations of school administrators and teacher leaders. School leaders who expect all teachers to collaborate provide specific and regular time for teachers to meet, require that teachers use this time to produce certain documents and evidence of student learning, and monitor this meeting time to ensure that progress toward team goals is being realized.

In schools that have effectively organized the faculty into professional learning communities, one of the first tasks each PLC has addressed is answering the first key question as outlined by DuFour and Eaker (1998): What is it we want our kids to learn? Schools that expect their students to learn the prescribed curriculum for each grade and subject have honest conversations about what is actually being taught. Often, they find that the actual curriculum and the intended curriculum are two very different things. Effective teams then go about the business of deciding with precision what should be taught at each grade level so that *The Outsiders* or *The Giver*, to offer but two examples, do not become books that are taught anywhere from 4th to 11th grade.

Another area in which overlapping from grade to grade occurs regularly and to the detriment of student learning is academic content vocabulary. Although it is true that certain terms such as "rhyme" in language arts or "multiplication" in math may well arise in language arts and math classes nearly every year, they should be formally taught and mastered at a specific grade level. After studying the work of Marzano (2004) and Marzano and Pickering (2005) related to building background knowledge and academic vocabulary, one middle school that was already thriving as a true professional learning community decided to identify 30 words in each content area at each grade level that teachers would be expected to teach and students would be expected to learn. As a result, a student who spent three years at the school would leave having mastered 90 academic vocabulary words in language arts, math, science, social studies, and even classes such as art, chorus, and band. Teachers referred to this as their "Thirty on the Wall" and each classroom had a poster displaying their Thirty on the Wall affixed to the same wall so that upon visiting any classroom in the school, one could find these academic content words in the same location. Whereas teachers previously took a somewhat random approach to teaching students key academic words and phrases, through collaboration they decided which words fit best at which grade level and agreed to "own" 30 strategically identified words at each grade level.

Until recently, what got taught from classroom to classroom was largely at the discretion of individual teachers. A student who had Mrs. Smith for American Literature could receive a completely different curriculum than the student taking American Literature with Mr. Johnson down the hall. One of the positive outcomes resulting from an increased focus on school accountability has been the understanding that such a system is patently unfair. Each student and parent should expect that the same curriculum will be taught whether their child ends up in Mrs. Smith's or Mr. Johnson's American Literature class. School leaders should expect that all teachers collaborate to ensure that agreement is reached in identifying precisely what must be taught at each grade level. Teacher styles and personalities do and should vary widely from classroom to classroom; our students are enriched when they learn from teachers with widely varying backgrounds, interests, and strengths. Differences in these areas are to be expected and even encouraged. At the same time, we must expect teachers to work together to determine what should be taught at each grade level and how learning should be measured.

Faculty Meeting Professional Development

Todd has stated on many occasions that his primary purpose in convening a whole faculty meeting is to have teachers more excited about teaching when they leave the meeting than they were upon arriving. We accomplish this goal by planning for two activities during all faculty meetings: celebrations and extremely brief professional development sessions. Previously, we mentioned several ways in which we celebrate school and teacher successes during faculty meetings. One other strategy we use to celebrate success that relates to expectations occurs at the very first faculty meeting of the year, typically during pre-planning, before the kids have even returned. As teachers begin to assemble, administrators and teacher leaders distribute 5 × 7 index cards to everyone assembled, including each other. The principal should ask each person in the room to think back to the previous school year and write about how they made a positive difference in the life of one student, describing in some detail the student, the situation, and the outcome. These should be written anonymously, without names placed on the cards. Teachers who are new to the school can write about a success they had at a previous school or during their student teaching experience. Next, collect the index cards and have teachers gather in small groups so that there are about ten groups total. Within these groups, redistribute the cards at random and have each person in each group take a turn reading what someone has written on the index card. Then, ask each group to pick their favorite example of making a difference in the life of a single student and read this example aloud to the entire staff. Starting off the school year by sharing ten or more examples of how we have made a positive difference in the lives of students is a powerful way to energize teachers for the new year. It is also a subtle way of establishing the expectation that our true purpose as educators is to make a difference in the lives of each individual student at our school. Finally, this is also an indirect form of professional development, in that teachers will be sharing strategies they used to succeed with certain students, oftentimes giving examples of how they managed to reach a reluctant learner.

Another way we reinforce our expectation that teachers provide professional development for each other during faculty meetings is by assigning small groups of teachers (or, after the first successful experience, soliciting volunteers) to "sponsor" a faculty meeting throughout the year. The assigned group can be a grade level, department, or professional learning community team. Their task is twofold: (1) provide a very short (perhaps 15–20 minute) presentation designed to address a specific aspect of teaching in which they have achieved success, and (2) provide the all-important light refreshments for the meeting. At a school where Jeff served as principal, the school leadership team "sponsored" the first faculty meeting and decided to adopt a baseball theme. They printed tickets for admittance to the meeting, placing these in mailboxes before the meeting and collecting them as teachers entered, later drawing one ticket out at random as a raffle winner. They provided peanuts, popcorn, and crackerjacks for snacks along with soft drinks. Then, wearing their favorite baseball cap and using the baseball analogy of a nine inning game, they presented nine specific strategies for establishing and maintaining effective classroom management. This proved to be a positive way to begin the faculty meeting and communicated expectations at two levels. First, teachers should help each other by sharing strategies to use in their classrooms. Through their presentation, they also were able to communicate school expectations for maintaining exemplary student behavior in all classrooms.

Another strategy to use at faculty meetings for teacher-led professional development is to ask each teacher to take an index card upon entering the meeting and write down a specific instructional or management challenge they are having in their classroom at the present time. Then, collect and redistribute the index cards. Have each teacher read the card they have received and write a possible solution to the challenge on the back of the index card. Pass cards along until at least three teachers have responded to the challenge with a solution in writing. To share, ask a few teachers to read the challenge on the card they are holding along with the three possible strategies for solving. Then, place all index cards on a table near the exit so that teachers can retrieve their original cards on the way out to see the suggestions offered by different colleagues.

We often limit teacher collaboration opportunities to formal, structured environments such as PLC meetings. By allowing time at each faculty meeting for teachers to collaborate informally by using ideas such as the three described above, we improve our school by sharing specific, practical ideas that have actually been used successfully at that school. Moreover, we are communicating our expectation that all teachers work together to identify those challenges that face us as well as solutions for overcoming these challenges.

Being There

One of the most important expectations to which all educators should adhere is simply to be there for their students and each other. This evidences itself in many ways throughout the school year, from expecting all teachers to be visible in the hallways during transitions, to expecting all teachers to devote time before or after school helping struggling students, to an often unspoken expectation that teachers maintain exemplary attendance. Almost every school we visit overtly emphasizes and recognizes student attendance, with periodic awards for perfect attendance. In these schools, teachers regularly cite poor student attendance as a contributing factor to poor individual student or whole school performance. Although teachers are quick to complain about a student who has missed, say, ten days a year, we rarely speak openly in our schools about teachers who miss ten days or more a year. It is clear that student attendance impacts student academic performance, yet it is equally certain that teacher attendance impacts student performance.

As is the case with most other variables relating to teacher behavior, our best teachers seem to have perfect or nearly perfect attendance each year, while our mediocre teachers consistently miss more days of school each year than they expect their students to miss. Administrators and teacher leaders must make explicit their expectations for teacher attendance. Admittedly, this is a delicate area; therefore, it is not surprising that in many schools, poor teacher attendance is not openly addressed. However, the issue is one that is so important to student and school success, that great educators find ways to set clear expectations for attendance and confront patterns of poor attendance when they arise. When the regular teacher is absent and a substitute is present, what are our expectations for student learning and student behavior that day? The truth is that even with the best substitute teacher filling in for a mediocre teacher, chances are good that students will learn less and behave worse than if the regular teacher were present. If we want our kids to learn as much as possible while exhibiting exemplary behavior, we must expect our teachers to have outstanding attendance. Take a minute and list the five best teachers at your school. We would be willing to wager that each of these five teachers has an outstanding track record in the area of their own attendance. Would students be better served if every teacher at the school had similar attendance performance? How, then, can we create a school culture in which it is expected that all teachers will maintain consistently outstanding attendance?

Of course, we can offer a variety of formal and informal incentives for teachers who have perfect attendance on a monthly and annual basis. This is a fun reminder to teachers at the school that teacher attendance is important in terms of student performance and valued within the school culture. We also must hold honest conversations with teachers who regularly fall short of our expectations in this area. No one can control certain health situations and there are years when even our most dedicated teachers experience a serious health setback or family tragedy that requires an extended amount of time away from the job. When this happens to our very best teachers who typically have stellar attendance, they usually feel worse about missing than we do. In such cases, school leaders should actually encourage these superstar teachers to take as much time as necessary, knowing that the circumstances are beyond their control and that they simply must be out. Yet, when patterns of excessive absences are noted, great administrators do not shy away from discussing this openly—albeit privately—with teachers.

In our informal studies of teacher attendance patterns, we have noted that a teacher who misses ten or more days one year typically misses ten or more days *each* year. At the same time, teachers who miss three or fewer days during any given year often miss three or fewer days *every* year. Such patterns would suggest that—to a certain extent—teacher attendance is related to choice, not circumstance. In speaking with teachers who have patterns of subpar attendance over a period of time, it is important to begin by letting them know that we realize most absences are simply beyond their control. Next, we should also remind them of how very important they are and that we believe they are the number one variable impacting their students' learning. We should discuss factual information, showing them exactly how many days they have missed over a period of time and perhaps comparing that to the average for all teachers within their department and at the entire school. We typically close such initial conversations by asking if they think students suffer when they are absent and by asking if there is anything we can do to help them so that their attendance can improve. Again, these are delicate situations and a number of factors must be considered when examining subpar teacher attendance, but holding honest conversations when a problem is detected in this area of teacher performance is a first step toward resolving a problem.

Establishing expectations for teacher attendance starts, of course, during the interview process. Describing the culture of the school as one in which teachers work very hard while at the same time having a great deal of fun is a good way to lay the groundwork for this. It makes perfect sense for an interviewing team to let prospective teachers know that at their school teachers pride themselves on being there each and every day for their students and for each other. We feel it is important to paint an honest picture of the school during the interview process so that candidates can consider if they are a good fit for the school. Toward that end, it is appropriate to share data with candidates about school achievement, student demographics, and even teacher attendance. For example, someone on the team might inform the potential teacher along the following lines: "Last year at our school, we had the highest teacher attendance rate of any school in the system. This is something we are very proud of, as we think it makes a positive impact on student achievement. Describe yourself in terms of your work ethic and your thoughts on how teacher attendance relates to student performance." In a subtle way, we have let the prospective teacher know that we value exemplary teacher attendance. This might even scare off a small percentage of less dedicated teachers and, if so, all the better. If, on the other hand, a teacher is hired after hearing this and subsequently exhibits attendance behaviors outside the school norm, we can remind them of the interview and the teacher's statement that they believed in being there every day for kids.

Even in a climate of ever-increasing analysis of all available data, we believe that the data related to teacher attendance remains an area that is often overlooked when examining school and student performance. Letting teachers know that they are the most important variable in determining how much students will learn in a school year sets the stage for expecting exemplary attendance on their part. We cannot succeed if our most important variable is not in place nearly every day of the school year. We must also systematically honor and recognize those teachers who consistently uphold our standards in this critical area. Finally, it is essential that school administrators model this as well. A principal who is out of the building on a regular basis cannot very well expect teachers to be there all the time. At the end of Jeff's first year of teaching, the school held an end-of-the-year banquet and arrived at the point when the principal said she wanted to recognize three people who had perfect attendance. Jeff's teaching teammate leaned over and whispered, "You are one of those!" to which he replied, "No; remember I had to take three hours off a few weeks ago to take care of that speeding ticket." (Alas, his penchant for blithely ignoring all posted speed limits continues to this day). The principal called up two teachers with perfect attendance and awarded them $100.00 provided by a business partner, which we certainly agree was an excellent gesture recognizing perfect attendance. Then, she called up an assistant principal for the same recognition and reward. The only problem was that this administrator had missed a week of school to accompany her husband on a business trip to Cancun just a few weeks before this ceremony. When a few teachers questioned this later, they were informed that she had accrued some "comp" time by working late and on weekends, an option not available to teachers at the school. As with most expectations, if we do not model the behavior we expect, we likely will not get it to the extent we desire. Teachers must model appropriate attendance for students, and administrators must do the same.

Staff Surveys

As a starting point for clarifying and creating school-wide expectations, school leaders can design a survey for all teachers to complete that aims to identify teacher attitudes regarding their expectations for the students they teach. Very few teachers consciously hold certain students to lower expectations than others, yet in an innocent and subconscious way, many well-meaning teachers with whom we have worked inadvertently communicate that they have differing sets of expectations for different groups of students. Until educators know where they are in terms of their expectations for all students, they cannot determine in which direction they must proceed. Any survey designed to gather data relating to teacher expectations should be tailored to the specific school administering the survey. However, a short survey with simple and direct statements such as the examples offered below should shed some light upon the issue of teacher expectations and serve as a starting point for open dialogue among the educators within the school:

(1) Most students in our school are capable of mastering grade-level learning objectives.
(2) Students at our school consistently behave appropriately.
(3) Students at our school perform academically at or above the state average.
(4) Teachers at our school believe that most students are able to master core content standards.
(5) My expectations for students influence how well they will perform academically.
(6) My expectations for students will influence how well they behave at school.
(7) Nearly all of my students will be at or above grade level by the end of the school year.
(8) Some of our students are destined to fail classes and/or not meet learning expectations.
(9) Students at our school behave better than students at surrounding schools.

(10) Teachers at our school are effective at establishing and communicating specific expectations for all students.

(11) All teachers at our school consistently adhere to school-wide expectations, enforcing them firmly, fairly, and consistently.

The above questions should serve merely as a starting point for any school interested in gauging teacher responses related to what we expect of the students and educators in our schools. Chances are good that themes will emerge in any such survey, providing an opportunity for all educators in the school to start discussions examining the expectations they hold for their students and each other.

Clarifying the C.O.R.E.: Expectations

The four dimensions of teaching, learning, and leading, which we both value above all others and which pervade all areas of the school, ultimately impacting its climate, culture, teacher morale, and student academic achievement, are *Communication*, *Observation*, *Relationships*, and *Expectations*. Educators committed to making a difference in the lives of students, each other, and the school itself must plan for excelling in each of these core areas. Of these four core factors, we close with our thoughts on expectations, but in many ways, this is the first value that must be addressed by every educator at the outset of every year. Much of what we believe in and much of our success as educators has been based on setting clear and lofty expectations for those with whom we work as we embark upon any venture and then building relationships with these people so that they will actually want to meet our expectations. If we do not make our expectations for students, teachers, and administrators explicit and fail to revisit these expectations periodically, the students, teachers, and administrators working in the school are less likely to work together for a common purpose and more likely to resort to working in isolation, perhaps even working at cross-purposes as they establish wildly varying expectations for their students and themselves. When faced with a lack of clarity regarding school-wide expectations, teachers tend to retreat to their classrooms, leading to a school that is, in reality, a collection of individual learning environments working in isolation under a common roof rather than a common set of values and expectations. In such a scenario, there may be as many sets of expectations as there are teachers in the school. In the great schools that we have visited and worked in, all educators within the school talk about their expectations regularly, arrive at consensus on core school-wide expectations for students and educators, remind each other of these commonly-held expectations, and adhere to these expectations consistently throughout the school year.

We believe that schools can improve student performance in terms of attendance, behavior, and academic achievement when they urge teachers and students to set high expectations for themselves—and monitor their adherence to these established expectations. When parents, teachers, and principals hold high expectations for students, students are more likely to expect more of themselves (Heck, Larsen, & Marcoulides, 1990). Principals play a key role in the area of expectations for all within the school. Austin (1979) found that the expectations principals hold for both student and teacher performance are positively related to student academic success. Teacher expectations may be even more powerful than principal expectations in this area, however. Teacher expectations tend to be self-fulfilling. If teachers expect students to behave well or perform well academically, they often do. Unfortunately, the inverse is true as well. At numerous schools we have visited, we have observed teachers who seem to expect students to behave poorly or to achieve at low levels. What is worse is that we have noticed these teachers are—subconsciously, one hopes—communicating these low expectations to the students they teach. According to Brophy (1983), teacher expectations affect student outcomes in a cyclical manner. At the outset of the year, teachers form differential expectations for students. Consistent with these differing expectations, they behave differently toward various students. These students, in turn, learn that they are expected to behave in a certain way, which affects their self-concept, motivation, conduct, and levels of aspiration over time. These student behaviors reinforce the teacher's initial expectations, ultimately resulting in high-expectation students achieving at or near their potential and low-expectation students gaining less than they might have if taught differently.

In examining teacher expectations for students and principal expectations for teachers, we find a great many similarities in terms of creating and communicating these expectations so that our ultimate outcome—higher levels of learning—is achieved. Whether discussing teacher expectations or principal expectations, effective schools follow these guidelines:

(1) *Establish and Communicate Expectations.* Great educators do this at the beginning of every school year. Teachers and administrators must discuss this openly during pre-planning days and agree on specific expectations that every staff member will have for students in terms of behavioral and academic performance. Great educators also reach consensus on what they will expect of each other. After reaching consensus and gaining a commitment from all educators in the school to adhere to these expectations, great schools identify a multitude of methods for communicating these school-wide expectations to all stakeholders throughout the school year, but particularly at the start of each new year.

(2) *Consistently Clarify, Reiterate, and Reinforce Expectations.* Great educators realize that simply having expectations and stating them at the beginning of the school year is not enough to make a difference. They find systematic ways to regularly clarify, reiterate, and reinforce the school-wide expectations agreed to at the beginning of the school year. They recognize teachers and students who meet and exceed school expectations consistently and address those within the school who are not meeting expectations. They do so fairly, honestly, and with an eye toward improving performance.

(3) *Serve as a Model.* Great educators model effective attitudes and practices in the area of expectations, serving

as their own best examples of desirable behavior. They act in a way that is consistent with their own and the school's expectations.

(4) *Monitor Commitment to School Expectations.* Great educators carefully monitor how students and staff are performing in terms of adherence to established expectations. Teachers monitor student performance, providing immediate and regular feedback to students. If a school-wide expectation is that wearing hats is not allowed in the building, every teacher on staff must monitor this and hold every student accountable for adhering to this school expectation. Administrators and teacher leaders monitor their own behaviors and act when they see that problems exist. If a school-wide expectation is that all teachers will be present in the hallways during transitions, every educator on staff will hold themselves and each other accountable for adhering to this school expectation.

Our purpose in the previous section of this chapter has simply been to offer a few simple, but specific, strategies that educators can employ to effectively and consistently establish, communicate, model, and adhere to school-wide expectations for student and educator behaviors, beliefs, and learning. Great educators clarify the core value of expectations at the outset of each year, with administrators and teachers working together to remind each other of important behaviors and practices in this area and addressing openly and honestly any concerns, setting a course for acting in strategic ways in order to embody this value throughout the school year to ensure optimal performance of all with whom they work.

Educators working in schools that are truly committed to high expectations for all students also have high expectations for each and every adult working in the building. Several years ago, Ron Edmonds (1986) committed to finding schools that were successfully educating *all* children, with the thought that if he could find even one in which all children were successful, then it was possible for any school to achieve similar results.

Evidence suggests that Edmonds was correct, as we have now identified a host of schools in which 90% of the student population members are of a minority race, 90% of the students are eligible for free or reduced lunch, yet 90% or more of all students are successful on standardized assessments. These schools have exhibited the will to educate each and every child so that they indeed learn at the highest levels possible. As with anything worthwhile that we do in education, accomplishing such a noble goal is not easy and setting high expectations is merely a starting point. Schools that make an impact in this area go beyond setting high expectations; they follow through on these expectations, turning them into commitments and insisting that all educators throughout the school adhere to and model school expectations for success.

Chapter Six

Keeping Your Eye on the Ball

The No Child Left Behind Act (NCLB) of 2001 reauthorized the Elementary and Secondary Education Act (ESEA), which stood as the primary federal law affecting education from Kindergarten through high school. NCLB was signed into law on January 8, 2002. Originally built on four principles—accountability for results, more choice for parents, greater local control and flexibility, and an emphasis on following best practices based on scientific research—NCLB is under increasing scrutiny at the time of this writing, a time when NCLB is scheduled for reauthorization and a presidential campaign is moving into high gear, bringing with it a great deal of talk on the part of every candidate about what should be done with NCLB and education in general. Since its inception, the merits of NCLB have been hotly debated on a daily basis by educators, parents, and politicians. Whether one is a fan or a foe of NCLB, one thing is certain: in the six years since it was signed into law, it has had a profound impact on the way we, as educators, conduct our business.

It is equally certain that laws relating to NCLB will change again, forcing educators to shift their focus once more. If anything is certain in the field of education, it is that change is certain. The world of education as we know it today will not exist in the same form tomorrow. As we said at the outset of this book, in matters of style, it is relatively painless and perhaps even beneficial to go with the flow. Yet, during such times of constant and inevitable change, great educators remain focused on core factors that consistently and steadfastly guide their daily actions, even when going with the flow of change.

Having strong core principles guiding our actions and behaving in strategic ways designed to fulfill these commitments are hallmarks of great educators. Such educators are able to thrive as professionals whether immersed in the era of open education, back to basics education, or standards-based education. Although they learn, grow, and adapt during each passing phase, they resolutely adhere to their own core educational values throughout, allowing any changes in style they undertake to be rooted in core beliefs, resulting in success for both the educator and the students with whom they work. For us, those four core factors are *Communication*, *Observation*, *Relationships*, and *Expectations*. Each of these four core factors is essential to school success—regardless of which way the educational pendulum is swinging. We have long ago accepted that constant changes in education are inevitable. However, to change and to change for the better are two different things.

Although we are strong advocates for continuously examining and reflecting on our practices with an eye toward fine-tuning what already works and changing that which does not, we are equally firm in our belief that successful change can only be undertaken when carried out by passionate educators who do so while guided by a core set of values. In the face of constant change, it is easy to become distracted, but it is simply imperative that we keep our eye on the ball, so to speak, with the "ball" being school success. We keep our eye on the ball that is school success by constantly examining how we can act in purposeful ways designed to increase student and teacher learning, working within the framework of the four core school success factors.

Coaching Clinics

In this book, we have attempted to share our own core educational values along with specific strategies for ensuring that we act in ways consistent with these principles despite inevitable tides of change. Previously, we mentioned that we both coached basketball early in our teaching careers. Somewhat surprisingly, perhaps, we found that we learned a great deal more about coaching when we attended coaching clinics than we did about teaching when we attended teacher in-services. At coaching clinics we attended, we listened to some of the most successful high school and college basketball coaches in the country share what worked for them. We listened attentively and scribbled notes furiously as coach after coach would go to the podium and share his or her ideas about zone defense, inbounds plays, full court presses, free-throw shooting, and conditioning drills. Each of these coaches would share something that was directly applicable to us as coaches and that we could take back to our school and implement the next day, if we wanted to. We have always thought that teachers and administrators should follow suit, offering "clinics" led by the very best educators in the field who simply stand up and share what has worked for them at their schools while giving explicit instructions for replicating at other schools. We hope that this book has provided practitioners at least a handful of strategies they can immediately employ at their schools in order to improve student and teacher performance.

Too often, it seems, we get swept up in the next educational fad that promises to solve all that ails our nation's schools. The truth is, of course, that no such program exists. Instead, it is our people who will solve the problems that face us—people committed to communicating clearly; observing and monitoring what is and is not working; building positive relationships with students, parents, and each other; and clearly establishing expectations for all stakeholders within the school community. Like the coaching community, we must identify those educators who are experiencing success in these four core areas and learn from them ways to enact similar strategies at our own schools aimed at positively impacting school success.

Proactive Versus Reactive

One of the most useful results of consistently acting in ways tied to core principles is that we tend to maximize the amount of time we are teaching and leading proactively, as opposed to reactively. The issue of student behavior is but one example in which it is clearly beneficial to focus on proactive behaviors rather than reactive behaviors in order to achieve the desired goal: better behaving students. When a teacher writes a discipline referral to an administrator and when the administrator assigns a consequence to the student for misbehavior, they are *reacting* to what has already occurred. At best, there is a chance that the student will learn a lesson and not misbehave again. However, in our experience, a more likely occurrence is that the teacher will soon write another referral and the student will soon be assigned an additional consequence. The students who tend to get written up seem unfazed by such consequences, limiting the effectiveness of such reactive behaviors on the part of teachers and administrators. Although we are staunch proponents of orderly schools and for holding students accountable for maintaining exemplary behavior, we also realize the limited efficacy of punishing students who misbehave. At times, of course, we are simply left with no other choice, and it is undoubtedly the proper course of action for both the misbehaving student as well as every other student and teacher in the building. Yet, for the vast majority of our students who want to succeed and tend to behave well most days, it is much more effective to promote the behaviors we desire through proactive measures.

By setting clear expectations for student behavior at the start of the year and then building positive relationships with our students—and their parents—each day thereafter, our very best educators seem to inspire kids to want to behave for them. When we take it a step further and observe kids behaving well and communicate this with their parents, we are again behaving in a proactive way which is much more likely to encourage continued good behavior as opposed to reacting negatively and after the fact to something that has already occurred. Although we use the example of student behavior to illustrate our point, the same holds true for student learning. Schools that are succeeding in terms of getting struggling students to meet academic standards act in proactive ways at the outset of each year, identifying those students with areas of academic needs and designing ways to meet these needs, rather than waiting until well into the school year and reacting to situations that may already be too far deteriorated to possibly improve. The key to behaving proactively rather than reactively is having a core set of values driving our actions as educators each and every day. By adhering to such core principles, great educators work in ways that inhibit student misbehavior or academic failure and instead foster student success.

The Case for the C.O.R.E.

In order to accomplish their goals and purposes, great educators develop within themselves and those with whom they work core factors that guide their actions on a daily basis and that are presumably very similar to the core factors shared by successful doctors, lawyers, bankers, and electricians. What makes each of these professionals the very best among their peers is not necessarily attributable to an exceptionally high degree of any technical skill; presumably, every doctor, lawyer, banker, and electrician is "highly qualified" in terms of technical expertise. Instead, it is the human relations skills they possess— and consciously practice—throughout each day on the job that sets them apart from other highly qualified professionals in their chosen field. While communication, observation, relationships, and expectations are all important in each of the professions named above as well as in probably every other walk of life, they are particularly necessary in order to serve as a great educator. We have stated repeatedly that, as educators, we are in the "people" business; we must excel at those skills that allow us to connect with people of all ages and backgrounds so that they are motivated to achieve at their highest level of potential. Great schools succeed if they are staffed by great teachers. Great teachers are ones who excel in the four core areas of communication, observation, relationships, and expectations.

The more teachers we have in a school who are committed to these four core factors, the greater the school will become. It is not enough to simply have pockets of excellence at each school in which a handful of teachers possess outstanding skills in these areas, while others do not. School leaders must create school cultures in which behaving according to the four core factors is the expected norm for all within the school. To achieve such a culture, schools must talk about these values at the beginning of each school year, discussing how they fared in each area the preceding year and how they can make sure they adhere to them even more consistently in the coming year. Working together, teachers and administrators should outline specific actions they will take throughout the year to uphold these four core factors and should incorporate these actions into their school improvement plans.

With the advent of No Child Left Behind has come the concept of "highly qualified" teachers. Ensuring that highly qualified teachers are in place in every classroom at every school in our country is a noble and proper goal. As a nation, we have improved in this area to the point that, in many school districts across the nation, it is almost a given that any teacher interviewing for a teaching position meets the requirements for being certified as "highly qualified." Again, this is good news for our schools and the students learning in them. Hiring teachers with well-developed knowledge and skills in content areas as well as pedagogy is essential, and we should be able to expect that any teacher applying for a position possesses this knowledge and skill set. On the other hand, we have observed many teachers who meet the standards for highly qualified status who were miserable failures as classroom teachers. While they possessed the necessary knowledge about teaching and their content area, they were woefully lacking in one or more of the four core areas.

We must continue to insist that our nation's educators are highly competent in terms of content knowledge and teaching techniques, yet we must also insist that—once in place—we do whatever it takes to ensure even higher levels of competency and quality in the areas of the four core factors for school success: communication, observation, relationships, and expectations. Creating a school culture in which every educator in the building consistently adheres to and excels in the four core areas is extremely hard. Yet it is also extremely simple in that it requires little in the way of theoretical knowledge, scientific research, or even advanced degrees. Instead, it comes down to consistent persistence, an indefatigable will on the part of every adult in the school to treat each student and each other in ways that will impact the success of the school in a powerfully positive way. A school characterized by educators committed to the four core factors provides a framework that sustains students and staff alike in times of constant change, instilling confidence in each other. Schools filled with confident educators and confident students are likely to make an impact that will be remembered. All schools make an impact on the students who attend them; great schools make a positive and lasting difference in the lives of students by keeping their eye on the ball: embodying the core factors of communication, observation, relationships, and expectations consistently and persistently.

References

The American heritage dictionary of the English language (4th ed.). (2000). Boston: Houghton Mifflin.

Austin, G. R. (1979, April). *An analysis of outlier schools and their distinguishing characteristics.* Paper presented at the annual meeting of the American Educational Research Association, San Francisco.

Barth, R. S. (1990). *Improving schools from within: Teachers, parents, and principals can make the difference.* San Francisco: Jossey-Bass.

Bissell, B. (1992, July). *The paradoxical leader.* Paper presented at the Missouri Leadership Academy, Columbia, MO.

Blackburn, B. R. (2007). *Classroom instruction from A–Z: How to promote student learning.* Larchmont, NY: Eye on Education.

Brook, J., Nomura, C., & Cohen, P. (1989). A network of influences on adolescent drug involvement: Neighborhood, school, peer, and family. *Genetic, Social, and General Psychology Monographs, 115(1),* 303–321.

Brophy, J. E. (1983). Research on the self-fulfilling prophecy and teacher expectations. *Journal of Educational Psychology, 75(1983),* 631–661.

Bryk, A. S. & Schneider, B. (2002). *Trust in schools: core resource for improvement.* New York: Russell Sage Foundation.

Bryk, A. S. & Schneider, B. (2003). Trust in schools: A core resource for school reform. *Educational Leadership, 60,* pp. 40–45.

Clark, R. (2003). *The essential 55: An award-winning educator's rules for discovering the successful student in every child.* New York: Hyperion.

Collins, J. (2001). *Good to great: Why some companies make the leap . . . and others don't.* New York: Harper Collins.

Cotton, K. (2003). *Principals and student achievement: What the research says.* Alexandria, VA: Association for Supervision and Curriculum Development.

Covey, S. R. (1989). *The 7 habits of highly effective people: Powerful lessons in personal change.* New York: Simon and Schuster.

DuFour, R. & Eaker, R. (1998). *Professional learning communities at work: Best practices for enhancing student achievement.* Alexandria, VA: Association for Supervision and Curriculum Development.

Edmonds, R. (1986). Characteristics of effective schools. In U. Neisser (Ed.), *The school achievement of minority children: New perspectives* (pp. 93–104). Hillsdale, NJ: Lawrence Erlbaum.

Ellis, E. C., Smith, J. T., & Abbott, Jr. H. A. (1979). Peer observation: A means for supervisory acceptance.

Fullan, M. (2001). *Leading in a culture of change.* San Francisco: Jossey-Bass.

Fullan, M. (2003). *The moral imperative of school leadership.* Thousand Oaks, CA: Corwin.

Goleman, D., Boyatzis, R. E., & McKee, A. (2002). *Primal leadership: Realizing the power of emotional intelligence.* Boston: Harvard Business School.

Gordon, S. P. (1991). *How to help beginning teachers succeed.* Alexandria, VA: Association for Supervision and Curriculum Development.

Hall, P. A. (2005). Communication is the key to effective leadership. *SEDL Letter, 17,* 12–16.

Heck, R., Larsen, T., Marcoulides, G. (1990). Instructional leadership and school achievement: validation of a causal model. *Educational Administration Quarterly, 26,* 94–125.

Hoerr, T. R. (Dec 2005/Jan 2006). The schoolhouse at midnight. *Educational Leadership, 63,* 86–88.

Hoerr, T. R. (Dec 2006/Jan 2007). Thanking your stars. *Educational Leadership, 64,* 90–91.

Howard, J. (1990). *Getting smart: The social construction of intelligence.* Lexington, MA: The efficacy Institute.

Kouzes, J. M. & Posner, B. Z. (1987). *The leadership challenge: How to get extraordinary things done in organizations.* San Francisco: Jossey-Bass.

Lencioni, P. (2005). *Overcoming the five dysfunctions of a team: A field guide for leaders, managers, and facilitators.* San Francisco: Jossey-Bass.

Lundin, S. C., Paul, N., & Christensen, J. (2000). *FISH! A remarkable way to boost morale and improve results.* New York: Hyperion.

Marzano, R. J. (2004). *Building background knowledge for academic achievement*. Alexandria, VA: Association for Supervision and Curriculum Development.

Marzano, R. J. (2007). *The art and the science of teaching: A comprehensive framework for effective instruction*. Alexandria, VA: Association for Supervision and Curriculum Development.

Marzano, R. J. & Pickering, D. J. (2005). *Building academic vocabulary: teacher's manual*. Alexandria, VA: Association for Supervision and Curriculum Development.

Marzano, R. J., Waters, T., & McNulty, B. A. (2005). *School leadership that works: From research to results*. Alexandria, VA: Association for Supervision and Curriculum Development.

McEwan, E. K. (2003). *7 steps to effective instructional leadership*. Thousand Oaks, CA: Corwin.

Mehan, H., Hubbard, L., & Villanueva, I. (1994). Forming academic identities: Accommodation without assimilation among involuntary minorities. *Anthropology and Education Quarterly, 25(2)*, 91–117.

National PTA (1997). National standards for parent/family involvement programs. Retrieved February 1, 2008, from http://www.ptasonline.org/kspta/national_standards.pdf

Pfeffer, J. & Sutton, R. I. (2000). *The knowing-doing gap: How smart companies turn knowledge into action*. Boston: Harvard Business School.

Reeves, D. B. (2006). *The learning leader: How to focus school improvement for better results*. Alexandria, VA: Association for Supervision and Curriculum Development.

Rosenthal, R. & Jacobson, L. (1968). *Pygmalion in the classroom: Teachers' expectations and pupils' intellectual development*. New York: Holt, Rinehart, and Winston.

Rutter, M., Maughan, B., Mortimore, P., Ouston, J., & Smith, A. (1979). *Fifteen thousand hours*. Cambridge, MA: Harvard University.

Saphier, J. (2005). Effort-based ability. In R. DuFour, R. Eaker, & R. DuFour (Eds.), *On common ground* (pp. 85–113). Bloomington, IN: National Education Service.

Schmoker, M. J. (2006). *Results now: How we can achieve unprecedented improvements in teaching and learning*. Alexandria, VA: Association for Supervision and Curriculum Development.

Sebring, P. B. & Bryk, A. S. (2000). School leadership and the bottom line in Chicago. *Phi Delta Kappan, 81(6)*, 440–443.

Smith, R. (2004). *Conscious classroom management: Unlocking the secrets of great teaching*. Fairfax, CA: Conscious Teaching.

Sommers, B. (2005). Communication is the key to effective leadership. *SEDL Letter, 17*, p. 28.

Tschannen-Moran, M. & Hoy, W. K. (1998). Trust in schools: A conceptual and empirical analysis. *Journal of Educational Administration, 36(3/4)*, 334–352.

Whitaker, T., Whitaker, B., & Lumpa, D. (2000). *Motivating and inspiring teachers: The educational leader's guide for building staff morale*. Larchmont, NY: Eye on Education.

Whitaker, T. (2003). *What great principals do differently: Fifteen things that matter most*. Larchmont, NY: Eye on Education.

Whitaker, T. (2004). *What great teachers do differently: Fourteen things that matter most*. Larchmont, NY: Eye on Education.

Zoul, J. (2006). *Improving your school one week at a time: Building the foundation for professional teaching and learning*. Larchmont, NY: Eye on Education.

Zoul, J. & Link, L. (2007). *Cornerstones of strong schools: Practices for purposeful leadership*. Larchmont, NY: Eye on Education.